TOWARDS A NEW CIVIC BUREAUCRACY

Lessons from Sustainable Development for the Crisis of Governance

Matthew J. Quinn

First published in Great Britain in 2022 by

Policy Press, an imprint of
Bristol University Press
University of Bristol
1–9 Old Park Hill
Bristol
BS2 8BB
UK
t: +44 (0)117 954 5940
e: bup-info@bristol.ac.uk

Details of international sales and distribution partners are available at
policy.bristoluniversitypress.co.uk

© Bristol University Press 2022

British Library Cataloguing in Publication Data
A catalogue record for this book is available from the British Library

ISBN 978-1-4473-5964-7 hardcover
ISBN 978-1-4473-5966-1 ePub
ISBN 978-1-4473-5967-8 ePdf

The right of Matthew J. Quinn to be identified as author of this work has been asserted by him in accordance with the Copyright, Designs and Patents Act 1988.

All rights reserved: no part of this publication may be reproduced, stored in a retrieval system, or transmitted in any form or by any means, electronic, mechanical, photocopying, recording, or otherwise without the prior permission of Bristol University Press.

Every reasonable effort has been made to obtain permission to reproduce copyrighted material. If, however, anyone knows of an oversight, please contact the publisher.

The statements and opinions contained within this publication are solely those of the author and not of the University of Bristol or Bristol University Press. The University of Bristol and Bristol University Press disclaim responsibility for any injury to persons or property resulting from any material published in this publication.

Bristol University Press and Policy Press work to counter discrimination on grounds of gender, race, disability, age and sexuality.

Cover design: Liam Roberts
Front cover image: iStock
Bristol University Press uses environmentally responsible print partners.
Printed in Great Britain by CPI Group (UK) Ltd, Croydon, CR0 4YY

To my parents

for showing me the life of reflective service to others

Contents

List of figures and tables		vi
Introduction		1
1	Framing the thinking	5
2	Governance and sustainable development as governmentality	14
3	Bureaucratic practice and governmentality	39
4	Lessons from governing for sustainable development	67
5	A new civic bureaucracy	93
Closing words		123
Appendices		125
References		146
Index		156

List of figures and tables

Figures
1.1	Foucault's governmentality and biopower	7
5.1	Civic and ecological governmentality	96
5.2	Language of partners about the Brecon Beacons	109

Tables
5.1	Relationships to nature	105
5.2	Farmer expressions of utility and feeling	106
5.3	Practice	120
5.4	Organization	121
5.5	Purpose and functions	122

Introduction

Context

This book owes its origins to my 30 plus years of practical experience – and oftentimes frustration – in attempting to pursue public policy on sustainable development as a civil servant in the UK, EU and UN. Despite those frustrations, I remain of the view that sustainable development, in the form of the Brundtland Report's ethical call to transformative action, has powerful lessons for how we might govern and, especially, for the future role of public bureaucracy.

My involvement with sustainable development as a bureaucrat began when I worked as part of the team which wrote the UK's first comprehensive environment strategy (*This Common Inheritance*) in 1990. My interest was then developed through the award of a Nuffield and Leverhulme international travelling fellowship to consider impacts of transport planning and policy upon the environment. This introduced me to international perspectives including the institutions of the World Bank and UN and brought me in contact with the New Zealand Resource Management Act. I also had the great privilege of learning from the differing perspectives of my main academic hosts: Professors Charles Vlek (RU Groningen), Peter Newman (Murdoch University) and Art Rosenfeld (Lawrence Berkley Laboratories). I was fortunate to apply this understanding in developing post-Rio Summit changes to UK land use planning in 1994 and to share this in EU and international fora.

A move away from the central government perspective in Whitehall – first to the (now abolished) UK government regional office in the South-West of England and then to the newly devolved government in Wales from 1998 – confirmed my growing feeling that there was great potential in more participative and localized engagement and decision-making. These approaches could reflect local circumstances and opportunities in a way that was near impossible in my central Whitehall experience. They could help to bring people together to consider and debate concerns in the round rather than from a narrow perspective and they could be supportive of grassroots action.

The 20 years in Wales were particularly formative. Here was a new institution in the making where the idea of government working in partnership with civil society and the pursuit of sustainable development had been set as guiding legal duties. This provided a formal test bed for learning about the relationship between existing bureaucratic practice, competing narratives of the role and form of governance, and the multifaceted challenge of sustainability. I am deeply indebted to all the colleagues both within the administration and in civil society who shared the ups and downs of that journey and together enriched our understanding. I think particularly of the contribution of the late Morgan Parry in his work at WWF Cymru and Countryside Council for Wales. Work in Wales also provided an opportunity to explore more fully the EU and UN administrative context when we helped to establish international networks of sub-national governments interested in sustainable development and sought to make the international case for the importance of a strategic but local and participative approach.

The cumulative experience left me with the abiding sense that there was a mismatch between the way public bureaucracy was organized and judged itself (or was judged) and the new challenges being faced by governance. It became increasingly clear to me that the concept of sustainable development itself presented fundamental challenges to the existing practice of public bureaucracies which were not being tackled. Instead, bureaucratic practice, and the external expectations placed upon it, came to distort, or constrain, the attempts to shape bureaucratic governance towards a more connected and participative framing of its role. Now, in the early 2020s, we are experiencing the wider crisis facing governance from right populism, a drift of politics towards seeing public servants as part of the problem rather than part of the solution and the huge challenge placed on public services by the global COVID-19 pandemic. I am drawn to reflect how the many creative and caring staff in the bureaucracies I served were constrained by custom and practice never to realize their wider potential as a positive force in society.

Thanks to the kind award of a Distinguished Visiting Fellowship from Cardiff University to undertake research at the Sustainable Places Research Institute (PLACE), I have had the opportunity over the past four years to ground my practical experience in the academic literature on governance, sustainable development and bureaucracy, and to conduct my own research. This has offered the chance to seek out more structural insights into my frustrations, and the successes along the way. I came to realize that academics look at practice for how it informs theory and I looked at theory as to how it could inform practice. I have sought to explore both perspectives, melding my own experience with theoretical framing, while aiming to allow the experience of working in bureaucracy to guide the insights. In this way I can hope to avoid the trap of narrow disciplinary perspectives and dispassion which were the very reason Max Weber categorized academia as a subset of bureaucracy and part of its same bounded, mechanical world.

I owe special thanks to Emeritus Professor Terry Marsden for his encouragement to pursue my academic journey in PLACE and to Professor Emerita Susan Baker for her generosity in supporting my tentative steps in exploring academic perspectives in her own expert field of governance for sustainable development (Baker, 2016). I am also very grateful for the assistance of my commissioning editor, Laura Vickers-Rendall, at Bristol University Press in shaping the focus of the book, and to my reviewers for their generous input. I owe a special indebtedness to Professor Emerita Harriet Friedmann for sharing the benefits of her wonderful transdisciplinary breadth in the suggestions on the initial typescript.

As a result of the COVID-19 pandemic, I completed my writing in the United States where I had the opportunity to experience bureaucracy, governance and civics US-style over the period of Black Lives Matter and the 2020 election. It has often felt extraordinary trying to complete a work which invokes the hopeful civic republican values and constitutionalism of the US Founding Fathers during such troubled times, and to see the way deeply conflicting views of governance have so shaped the responses to the pandemic for the worst. I have my wife Kathryn to thank for helping me to bring the draft to completion despite such difficult circumstances.

This book represents an initial fruit of academic reflection on my chosen profession of public servant. It seeks to answer questions that arose repeatedly in my practice:

- how potentially transformative narratives of governance, sustainable development and bureaucracy are dragged back to a narrow economic and managerialist focus;
- how the practice of public bureaucracy and the recent focus of reform efforts has served to constrain moves towards fresh approaches to governance; and
- whether innovations in governing for sustainable development can point the way to a different future for a public bureaucracy which can meet 21st-century needs.

While there has been academic interest in the role of institutions and networks in sustainability, often focused on international work, bureaucracy itself has not generally been explored as a distinct factor in the persistence of unsustainability. Indeed, bureaucracy has been deeply neglected in the study of political philosophy more generally and its ideas of the operation of the state (Heath, 2020). Yet, bureaucracy matters because it is the mechanics of governance. It provides the day-to-day experience of government as the main interface for citizens. It holds the ring on engagement and consultation with civil society. It has a set of tools to judge how advice and decisions should be crafted. It proposes solutions to issues identified by politicians. It creates the processes, forms and audit requirements that citizens face in seeking support or answers. The way it operates shapes how governance works, what governance values and promotes, and how governance is viewed in society.

I aim to bring a practitioner eye to bear on the potential and constraints of bureaucracy, remembering what a closed book public administration can be to the outsider. As Tom Burke once confided when he joined the UK Department as a specialist advisor after years as a green activist: "For years I have been trying to put together the jigsaw of how administration works and now someone has given me the lid to the jigsaw box." I trust some of what I write may serve as a similar guide, at least to the contexts within which I have worked.

Too often when I read recommendations about public bureaucracy or governance in academic articles they fall foul of an innocence or broad assumption about the nature of public administration, governance and politics. The hard sciences appear stuck in a rationalist, technocratic trap where better facts speak for themselves, or in a centralized control model in which legislating for specific protections or targets creates change by itself. Some social science fares little better, especially writing on public administration and politics, which can appear little touched by critical theory and stuck with management dogmas, a focus on principal-agent theory of the relationship between the political and the bureaucratic, or a narrow focus on efficiency rather than addressing questions of bureaucracy's purpose and its potential wider civic impact.

Dominant critique of bureaucracy has not been concerned with how its practice and narratives serve to bound the scope, methods and purpose of governing but instead by arguments about inefficiency of delivery of services, drawn from economics and management theory. Most recently, fashionable reforms have explored not the role of public bureaucracy in society but how to make it a more focused and slimmed-down delivery vehicle of government services and goals, responsive to the public as consumers of services, using marketization and choice of provider and guided by specific and narrowly drawn delivery targets.

This model of bureaucratic organization is now facing the challenges of sustaining planetary health – seen in issues from climate change to pandemics – while addressing increasing public discontent with existing democratic systems. Public bureaucracy is operating in a political context of neoliberal views of the limited role of the state in society, a populist lauding of domination over others, and post-truth values that deny expertise as legitimation for the exercise of power. Together these offer existential threats to democratic governance and to ideas of public service. I hope that the radical possibilities for a future civic bureaucracy shown by innovation in sustainable development governance may inform discussion of the transformation that will be needed towards more engaging and just forms and tools of bureaucratic governance – a transformation that can truly address the fundamental challenges of this new century.

1

Framing the thinking

All general theories must, as theories, keep modestly in the background, not in open argument only, but even in our own minds.

Woodrow Wilson

Introduction

Academic and political approaches to sustainable development, governance and public administration reflect a diverse range of values and disciplinary lenses. This makes it nigh impossible to find a common theoretical frame for exploring the question of what lessons sustainable development governance has for bureaucracy. Any single framing risks ignoring important debates and viewpoints. Applying theory also risks the ire of the Anglo-Saxon distrust of theory, a distrust captured in Woodrow Wilson's opening quote to the chapter, but a lack of theory can be very unhelpful to consistency of approach and the ability to reflect. In preparing this book, however, I have been drawn to a set of writers on governance who seem to speak most clearly to the concerns I found in my bureaucratic practice.

Of the modern authors, I have focused on Michel Foucault's analyses of technologies of power and domination and on Phillip Pettit's presentation of the aim of civic republican governance as the minimization of domination over others. Pettit and Foucault appeal because they both recognize governance as a dynamic process and acknowledge the significance of the minutiae of process that are the stuff of bureaucracy, not just the grand political sweep.

I pair the modern voices with historic ones, notably Max Weber, with his interest, not so dissimilar from Foucault's, in the controlling power of bureaucracy, and Woodrow Wilson, the academic 28th US president, with his sense of bureaucracy as a positive force for civic good. I have also been hugely in the debt of key writers on green governance and governance for sustainable development, particularly James Meadowcroft, whose article 'Who's in charge here?' (Meadowcroft, 2007) arguably remains the clearest exposition of the complex issues around governing for sustainable development, and John Dryzek who has been in the vanguard of thinking about dialogue and deliberative or discursive democracy as a pathway to realizing sustainable development (Dryzek, 2010).

Critical theory

Michel Foucault appeals because he focuses on the systemic nature of governance and how it is shaped and reiterated over time. This historical and practice-based view helpfully serves to bring into play many of the potential lenses through which the role of bureaucracy might be viewed.

Foucault's central conception of governance is a constant interplay of practice and justifying narratives in which power is not taken, so much as established in different equilibria. Here, power is seen as an essentially creative force which is everywhere, from day-to-day interpersonal interactions to global politics. The question for Foucault is how power is applied and legitimized through narratives and structures which create the social context within which it can be exercised. This is interesting in the context of bureaucracy because it is both constrained by its context and in turn constrains others by its resulting practice.

In the historical, genealogical analysis presented by Foucault in his lectures at the College of France (Foucault, 2008), he tracks the emergence of the modernist world and nation state as a period of the rise of 'biopower' (*biopouvoir*). This is a particular combination of mechanisms and narratives which have the effect of ordering the population, often through forms of exclusion of certain groups or activities. This combination has political economy as its main object and uses forms of discipline to enable it. The art of exercising governance in such a system, using specified apparatus – or *dispositifs* – Foucault termed 'governmentality':

> [T]he ensemble formed by the institutions, procedures, analyses and reflections, the calculations and tactics that allow the exercise of this very specific albeit complex form of power, which has as its target population, as its principal form of knowledge political economy, and as its essential technical means apparatuses of security. (Foucault, 1991, 102)

Figure 1.1 seeks to presents Foucault's framing of governmentality and biopower graphically. Here, the combination of repetition of practices and historical decisions and framings drive societal and political interaction over time in a systemic, self-reinforcing dynamic. Narratives, institutions, procedures, punishments and the physical organization of the use of land together constitute 'technologies of power' which continually shape how we may live. They create 'regimes of truth' based on approved forms of knowledge-power and a 'milieu', or social and physical environment, which prescribes what is possible: 'a system of ordered procedures for the production, regulation, distribution, circulation and operation of *statements* ... linked in a circular relation with systems of power which produce and

Figure 1.1: Foucault's governmentality and biopower

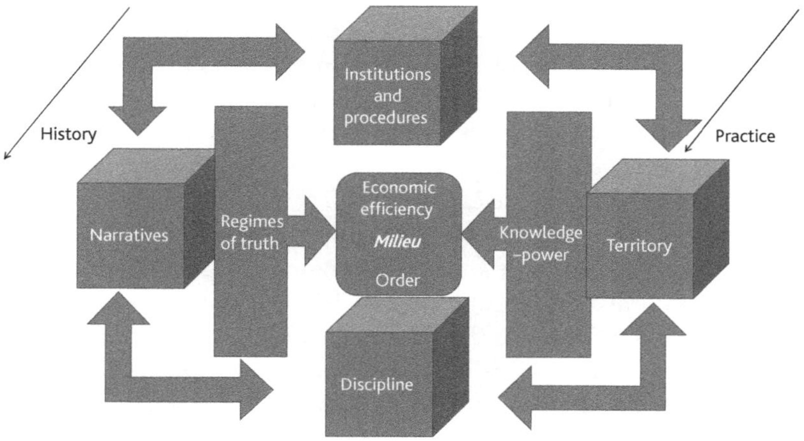

sustain it, and to effects of power which it induces and which extend it' (Foucault, 1977).

In the book, I seek to use this frame of historical narratives and of practice to understand how bureaucracy has been shaped and in turn shapes what is considered possible. This prompts reflection that the characteristics we casually think of as normal, inevitable and useful in governance and bureaucracy may be anything but.

Foucault's concepts and associated methods offer a suitably broad canvas to explore the themes of the book. His approach to discourse as 'discursive formations' enables a mapping of the partial narratives which shape and inform governance. His approach to genealogy helps to explore historical ideas which have shaped both our assumptions on bureaucracy and the nature of its practice. His understanding of the role of institutions, procedures, discipline and territorial organization (which constitute a particular type of ordering of what is possible) informs the analysis of the present practice of bureaucracy and the nature and impact of its constraint on change. Foucault's conception of 'the governance of things' also speaks to the contested issue of what should be the human relationship with environment and nature – an issue central to ethical conceptions of sustainable development. His analysis of forms of power also speaks directly to Max Weber's formative analysis of bureaucracy in *Wirtschaft und Gesellschaft* (Weber, 1922, Part 3 Chapter VI), an analysis whose arguments still underpin both justification and critique of bureaucracy's practice.

Foucault came late in his talks to express the idea that the purpose of governance, on a continuum of scales from the international to the personal, should be a moral goal to 'minimize domination over others'. To develop this demands analysis of the *rules, techniques and ethos* of governing:

I don't believe there can be a society without relations of power, if you understand them as means by which individuals try to conduct, to determine the behaviour of others. The problem is not of trying to dissolve them in the utopia of a perfectly transparent communication, but to give oneself the rules of law, the techniques of management, and also the ethics, the ethos, the practice of self, which would allow these games of power to be played with a minimum of domination. (Fornet-Betancourt et al, 1987, 119)

And, between the two, between the games of power and the states of domination, you have governmental technologies – giving this term a very wide meaning for it is also the way in which you govern your wife, your children, as well as the way you govern an institution. The analysis of these techniques is necessary, because it is often through this kind of technique that states of domination are established and maintain themselves. (Fornet-Betancourt et al, 1987, 130)

Non-domination and ecology

Foucault associates governmentality with the growth of the modern industrial, urban economy and the need for an ordered, bounded and economically efficient system to support mass democracy. This system draws its analogy from the world of mechanization and Fordist production in which competition, division of labour, predictability and uniformity are key.

Ecology offers a competing analogy. This is one of complex interacting systems which are not based in uniformity and control but in self-regulating diversity and interaction. While the Darwinian sense of nature as red in tooth and claw and the notion survival of the fittest has fed the economic narrative of the centrality of competition, from an ecological perspective, such competition takes place within systems which sustain equilibria. Total domination would mean the collapse of the system. There is increasing understanding of the extent to which nature has collaborative structures, such as the networks of communication across the forest floor. Such an ecological perspective underpins concepts of limits to growth and the need for sustainable development. This is why these are so challenging for existing governance and the practice of bureaucracy which were designed on a different analogy to achieve different purposes. The recognition of the concept of the Anthropocene indicates how far social and economic systems have come to dominate the natural systems which are essential to existence. As Dobson puts it:

ecologism throws into relief a factor – the Earth itself – that has been present in all modern political ideologies but has remained invisible, either due to its very ubiquity or because these ideologies' schema for description and prescription have kept it hidden. Ecologism makes the Earth as physical object the very foundation-stone of its intellectual edifice, arguing that its finitude is the basic reason why infinite population and economic growth are impossible and why, consequently, profound changes in our social and political behaviour need to take place. (Dobson, 2007, 12)

Non-domination and civics

The idea of ecology as a competing analogy for how governance systems might work and Foucault's comments on minimizing domination over others leads us to the consideration of the potential civic purpose of governance systems and the role of bureaucracy. This would be an aim for the system to sustain and enhance democratic life, supporting an inclusive and plural society. This is an emancipatory idea which runs as a bifurcation through the literature of governance and bureaucracy in the division between civic (social and ecological) and economic efficiency narratives of purpose and organization. The political science tradition closest to governance as civics is civic republicanism, whose focus is sustaining democratic government by promoting civic ethics through the application of the rule of law and the detailed design of institutions of government. Philip Pettit's writings on modern civic republicanism offer principles that can inform a practical response to Foucault's call (Pettit, 1997). Pettit advocates a civic republicanism that sets non-domination as the guiding principle and goal of governance. This offers a potential alternative test for the legitimacy and form of bureaucratic action and organization. Drawing on historical and contemporary thinking, Pettit works through some of the practical implications of a goal of non-domination for the nature of governance. Like Foucault, Pettit is interested in the minutiae of technologies of power: 'The ideal of freedom as non-domination suggests that pedestrian matters of institutional design are of the first importance; it argues for a gas-and-water works version of republicanism' (Pettit, 1997, 280).

Civic republicanism speaks directly to the issues I encountered in governing for sustainable development. The global ethic of sustainable development set out in the introduction to the founding document of sustainable development in public policy, the 1987 World Commission on Environment and Development (the Brundtland Report (WCED, 1987) is essentially a civic republican one – a call to participation, collaboration and civic virtue to develop a new understanding of what it means to develop. The connection between green governance and civic republicanism has been expressly drawn in works by John Barry (Barry, 2008, 2012) and by Robyn Eckersley (Eckersley, 2004). The question remains whether this concept can be operationalized as a guiding and legitimating narrative that can provide a new focus for governing, and whether its practical application can provide for bureaucracy a new form of neutrality to replace the present one that is based in bounded rationality, economic efficiency and service to the government of the day.

Civic republicanism has a striking contemporary resonance in seeing the role of governance as primarily a civic bulwark to sustain the existence of republics against the threat of oligarchy or despotism. The legitimacy for use of power and rules is judged not against economic efficiency but against whether they can sustain the unity of a pluralistic democratic state. This was thinking which greatly influenced the US Founding Fathers in framing the Constitution and is echoed in the oft-quoted response of Benjamin Franklin, when asked about the outcome of the Constitutional Convention, that the discussions had produced 'a republic – if you can keep it'. At a time of mounting right populism and hostility to democratic values, this is a timely reminder from history.

Civic republicanism is a broad conception but is chiefly focused on how government, and now governance, is organized and whether that promotes a connected, thoughtful and diverse polity in which proposals can be readily contested. It does not presuppose a particular political ideology and can be consonant with, and indeed encourages, different political approaches and ideas provided they do not threaten that conception of the republican polity. Only strongly libertarian or totalitarian stances would fail the test as in essence being opposed to government and to plurality respectively. Civic republicanism is not without its critics. It has been viewed as a counsel of perfection inappropriate for the modern combative age. Its call for dialogue and civics can seem naïve in current times and it does not in itself offer a precise recipe for change. Yet civic republicanism has long been part of the fabric of constructing democratic states. It persists in the importance of the rule of law rather than arbitrary decisions (Harrington's 'an empire of laws not men' [Harrington, 1656]); Montesquieu's formal separation of powers between the legislature, the judiciary and the executive (Montesquieu, 1949) to provide checks and balances so no part should dominate the others, and Madison's advocacy of a constitutional federalized democracy in which plurality and distinctiveness of places can be recognized and respected, and can drive new understandings (Hamilton et al, 2009).

Historically, minimizing domination over others has been limited by who or what counts as a legitimate 'other'. In western writings since the Enlightenment, and still reflected in much of society's organization, the other who deserves not to be dominated is simply a property-owning White male human citizen. This is perpetuated as a form of domination by an almost Darwinian competitive narrative that legitimates the exercise of domination by the 'fittest' – the successful, the rich, the charismatic, the privileged or the 'true' people. It is a narrative that has also seen nature as something to be mastered and exploited (Kolodny, 1975). But the civic republican notion of 'we the people' does not need to be so constrained. Concern for the protection of minorities and alternative viewpoints can be seen as lying at its heart. It continues to resonate in US political life, even in difficult times, where the idea of freedom as 'minimizing domination over others' offers a contrast to the classical liberal conception of freedom as 'minimization of interference' with the individual. That is, drawing an analogy from the COVID-19 pandemic that began in 2020, the contrast between the duty to wear a mask to protect others and the right not to wear a mask to please oneself.

Considering bureaucratic governance in the administrative state as a potential force for non-domination and plurality, rather than playing its role as an instrument of domination and uniformity, can help to point to the systemic change needed to the detailed ways in which the procedures, rules and narratives of bureaucracy serve to normalize certain forms and foci of consideration, and reward or punish certain behaviours.

The challenges

The challenge of sustainable development presents a fundamental question for the focus of the governance of liberal democracies that is on a level at least as challenging if not more than that faced in the interwar years. The challenges of those years led down two pathways – to totalitarianism which swept away the old state and its careful checks and balances, or to the recognition that the state needed to adapt to address the limitations and impacts of the market economy on civil society. By considering the new challenges of sustainable development and its governance needs, I hope to establish a picture of an alternative approach to the role of bureaucracy. This would move it from its increasingly ill-fated focus on the application of 'knowledge-power' of technocratic control and uniformity for economic efficiency. It would instead become enabler of transformatory civic dialogue and support a deeper understanding of, and positive agency in, the complex socio-ecological systems in which we exist. Such a new framing is not only important for sustainable development but also for sustaining democratic life.

Right populism and the death of knowledge-power

The most successful political harnessing of narratives in reaction to the 21st century's socio-ecological challenges has come not from civic republicanism, sustainable development or the academic concept of the Anthropocene, but from right populism.

The response of many of political, societal and governmental institutions to the first years of this century has been to try to assert a vision of past values – of industrialization, narrow nationalism, 'jobs and growth' or religious fundamentalism. Whether in the UK vote to leave the European Union, the growth of nationalist movements across the world or the rhetoric of the right in America, the political appeal is essentially to a nostalgia for past times with simple slogans of past glories and old values.

For all the nostalgia, the changes of the 20th century can be also seen as having been for the better. Worldwide, living standards and conditions, life expectancy and local environments, security and equality have significantly improved overall (United Nations, 2015). But the beneficiaries of that change are unevenly spread, with in-country income inequalities growing rather than narrowing since the turn to neoliberalism, and the relative certainties around employment for life and clear status in society that was offered by the old industrial systems have gone, leaving many people feeling uncertain or angry. The change to the modern world has also brought global environmental challenges for the first time. Our economies together produce more waste than the earth can absorb, leading especially to the serious challenges of climate change and to competition, sometimes even war, over scarce resources. Like the closely related issues of global trade, movement of people and security, these are beyond the scope of the individual nation states which are still presented as the basic unit for the protection of the citizen.

The appeal to nostalgia typically treats the main aspects of change as the causes of the problems people perceive in society. Thus, the need for action on climate change is denied or treated with scepticism as being simply a way to undermine the old industrial base and reduce freedoms. Immigration is painted as the main reason for loss of employment in local economies. International institutions are pictured as interfering with national self-determination rather than regulating global concerns.

Structuring the analysis

The book applies Foucault's genealogical approach to explore how narratives of governance, sustainable development and bureaucracy and their associated practice, rules, controls and institutions create 'regimes of truth' – the unspoken assumptions about what is normal or desirable. It paints a picture of the contested nature of these truths in which there is a bifurcation in which a democratizing strand of thought is repeatedly drawn back to a traditional focus on economic efficiency.

Alongside the brief portraits of contested academic and political thinking, the discussion draws heavily on the varying pursuit of sustainable development governance over my career and especially the 20 years of devolved Welsh Government in the UK. Using cases drawn from my own experience, supported by discussions with key actors in public policy efforts, and citing associated law and public policy documents, the book illustrates the way in which the emancipatory and controlling narratives of governance, sustainability and bureaucracy have played out in practice. It reveals how measures intended to deliver non-domination and reflexivity in governance and bureaucracy can be distorted or stifled by technologies of power associated with very different narratives.

The book considers the lessons from experimentation in sustainable development governance as a response to the stifling of emancipatory intent. The experience of these innovations reveals issues for the design and repurposing of future bureaucratic endeavour. Finally, the book suggests a potential framework for governmentality which draws on the socio-ecological aim of governance as non-domination and sketches the nature and legal framework for a purposive and liberated public bureaucracy. This civic bureaucracy, I argue, would move from the focus on uniformity and control that sustains a particular form of political economy to become an enabler of long-term change towards a more inclusive, diverse, sustainable and creative future.

2

Governance and sustainable development as governmentality

> The real world of interlocked economic and ecological systems will not change; the policies and institutions concerned must.
> *Our Common Future*, World Commission on Environment and Development

Personal reflection

Newly minted in 1986 after graduating from college, I joined the civil service with a smattering of governance knowledge gleaned from my reading at university of Plato and Aristotle and the Enlightenment moral philosophers. I arrived with a naïve sense of my future work as the objective balancing of societal needs.

My formal introduction to UK governance, such as it was, came with my induction training as a fast-stream civil servant. I dare say my French colleagues, who pass through L'Ecole Nationale d'Administration, receive a more philosophical perspective, but our British training was one of process and order. The training module 'Parliament, Government and the Civil Service' gave a formal view of the respective relations and a practical sense of how to navigate them through case examples and talks by senior, recently retired guest speakers. At no point did we spend time on considering what governance was for – our role was simply to support the process as impartially as we could. There was also nothing, as I can recall, about the public or stakeholders, although we did interestingly receive training in presentation skills. The remaining focus was on the core practice skills of evidence-based advice – economics (especially cost–benefit analysis) and statistics, business and public accountancy and the basics of avoiding judicial review of decisions. It was very much functional not reflective training in keeping with the Anglo-Saxon suspicion of theory called upon by Woodrow Wilson in his 1887 paper on the study of administration (Wilson, 1887).

It was only as I began work in my first civil service role that the nature of governance became clearer. First the centrality of networks and lobbies was obvious. Developing policy meant working externally with others. For me, doing this felt important both to understand the issues fully and emotionally, rather than abstractly, and to enable policy making to be about going on a journey together with stakeholders. In London, this was essentially about working with the headquarter teams of key business, professional and environmental groups. This was especially clear in my responsibilities for land use planning policy where major development interests and professional bodies dominated debate. It also taught me about the dynamics of agencies: it was not enough to issue new guidance, you also had to take the Planning Inspectorate with you to ensure the guidance was implemented in subsequent planning appeals. Parliament, by contrast, was a very distant beast from my Whitehall existence. It surfaced when a minister had to leave a meeting to vote, in the occasional parliamentary written or oral question which came your way, or the very rare chance that you had to take through a piece of primary legislation.

As well as lobby interests, ministers were very present for us in shaping the process of policy making. A key learnt skill as a new civil servant was to present issues in a way which was likely to command official and political support – the formal policy submission was essentially a 'pitch'. Evidence-based policy making and impartiality were still formally the requirement, but it was the way the immediate goal of governance was framed at any one time – a focus more on economy, society or equality – which determined what counted as *relevant* evidence. When evidence was sometimes stretched or applied selectively, this was humorously termed 'policy-based evidence making', something to be frowned upon yet acknowledged as a reality. This meant that a central part of bureaucratic practice was constrained by predominant narratives of the role of public administration which shifted and co-existed over time. The bureaucrat's required sensitivity to the political context as a servant of the government of the day is an important factor in understanding how public bureaucracy is never really objective but exercises discretion as to what it offers as acceptable options within a given context, or *milieu* in Foucault's terms.

I wrote about these policy development processes rather innocently in my first academic contributions. There were two chapters setting out the practices of developing planning policy in the late 1990s for edited academic textbooks (Quinn, 1996, 2000). More critically, when I had moved outside of Whitehall, I weighed the case for people-based versus evidence-based policy making in a paper published from a symposium talk (Quinn, 2002).

I was fortunate in my career to have the stimulus of working in two newly formed structures. First came the late-lamented Government Office for the South-West, created in 1994 in a decentralizing spirit and abolished in 2011 in an austerity-themed push for small government. From there I joined the Welsh Government in 1998, the year in which it was being established as part of the UK devolution programme. I stayed there for the rest of my bureaucratic career during which time Wales was progressively awarded additional powers, although remaining a creature of UK law rather than enjoying any constitutional protections for its status. In both cases, the creation of a new body provided an opportunity to question the way things were done. Both bodies were enabled to emerge from cautious branch office mentalities to begin to explore the possibilities of new ways of working and engagement with the wider world, testing the edges of the bounded rationality of centralized bureaucracy. These appointments outside the central government in Whitehall brought wider contact with civil society and the opportunity to build relationships. In both the South-West of England and Welsh cases there was a sense across administration and civil society that the new arrangements could be about building a distinct new approach, not just institutionally but also through the ways of working. There was the possibility of governance as open network rather than controlling hierarchy. The spirit, and often the narrative, was a democratizing one of partnership with civil society.

The first period of Welsh devolution also saw an accidental experiment in governance. The original legal model for Welsh devolution was what was often pejoratively called 'a local authority on stilts'. This provided no separate executive and legislature, but a single body run by committees of Assembly members. It was modified in its final incarnation to give executive authority to Assembly secretaries (effectively, and soon afterwards, renamed as ministers) but the single body structure remained. Ministers were both answerable to and also members of the committees. For the first term at least, taken in combination with the impact of minority and coalition governments that were rarities in the UK and the commitment to societal partnership, the civil servants found themselves working actively for the first time both with ministers and with the Assembly members as well as wider civil society interests. This was a bureaucracy serving the effectiveness of the polity not just the government of the day. This unusual experience is perhaps best captured in the general briefings that my team provided for the first administration. These briefings gave a pen portrait of issues in Wales and were provided equally to Assembly members and to ministers, but only the ministerial version included sections on policy. In discussions for the preparation of this book, many colleagues looked back with some fondness on this wider role in supporting the polity and the very different spirit of a more collaborative democracy. The accidental experiment in the bureaucratic role was quickly dismissed, however, as 'breaking governance 101' and when the opportunity came for a fresh Government of Wales Act, the model was replaced by a traditional executive–legislative split with the bureaucracy serving the executive alone.

Contested governmental concepts

The world into which I entered had a long backstory – rooted chiefly in Enlightenment liberal political philosophy and classical economics. The role of the state was not so very far removed from its 18th- and 19th-century origins as the guarantor of property, security and liberty to allow the accumulation of individual wealth. As civil servants we had a broad regard to the 'public interest' but exactly what that denoted was rather less clear and was largely determined through economic tests and utilitarian concepts of increasing total benefits. After two world wars and the introduction of welfare safety nets, the state had taken on much more responsibility for regulating the market economy and addressing its limitations – or as I learnt to term them, 'externalities' – but economic efficiency was still the focus and legitimation.

My public service career tracked the adoption and exposition of two contemporary governmental concepts that remain both relevant and contested to this day. These emerged from the uncertainties of the end of the '*trente glorieuses*' period of post-war Keynesian welfarism in the 1960s and 1970s when counterculture and anti-war movements, the rise of awareness of the Global South and the civil rights movement shook the complacency of the politics of post-war consumerism, a complacency summed up in the US Democratic Party's 1952 election campaign slogan 'You've never had it so good'. The two new challenging concepts were sustainable development (updating the notion of development) and governance (in lieu of government). Both terms appeared full of emancipatory promise and attracted me to build my bureaucratic career path in the broad field of sustainable development governance.

Over that same period another response emerged to the cultural and political uncertainties of the 1970s in the form of what was first known as supply-side economics, later Reaganomics and Thatcherism, and finally as neoliberalism. This saw the answer to contemporary uncertainties as a rolling back of the paternalism perceived in the welfare state and the Keynsian economics of demand-side adjustments. It took the focus back to the classical liberal view of government as a kind of necessary evil (Hobbes, 2005). This was expressed in deregulation, privatization and marketization, welfare reduction, a war on trade union power and in tax and fiscal policies which focused on addressing inflation rather than employment and on reducing the redistribution of wealth.

The tension and interplay between the apparent emancipatory promises of sustainable development and of governance and the competing mechanisms and narratives of neoliberalism were perhaps the meat of our bureaucratic struggles. In seeking to pursue governance for sustainable development in my various roles and teams, I was often reminded of my welfare officer father's sad comment after returning home from study for his certificate in social work: "I always thought I was an agent of social change and now I realise I am probably an agent of social control." The core of the book and of its exploration of a future for public bureaucracy as a virtuous civic force is this tension for the bureaucrat within the system in which they operate between the potential of emancipatory change and the way in which it is dragged back both by competing narratives and by rules and processes.

This chapter explores the competing narratives of governance and of sustainable development to understand how they create regimes of truth which set the context for public bureaucracy and determine how it comes to exercise or mitigate tools of domination.

Governance

In academia, and in public policy, governance is the term used to describe the process and nature of governing which involves a range of societal actors rather than simply government itself. This modern use of the term 'governance' differs from the traditional term 'government' in recognizing and endorsing the role played by different actors and external relationships in governmental steering of society. This meaning is distinct from its use as a term for the internal ruling processes of businesses or institutions. In recent literature and in public policy, the term governance is typically used descriptively of the nature of multi-stakeholder processes or normatively as how governing should be undertaken. Foucault uses governance as a nested term which he applies to all power relationships from the supranational to the interplay of individual relationships. Its 'notoriously slippery' nature (Pierre and Peters, 2000) can be seen in the range of *Oxford English Dictionary* descriptions:

OED 'governance'

1a The office, function, or power of governing; authority or permission to govern
1b A person, body, or thing that governs
2a Conduct of life or business; mode of living; behaviour, demeanour
2b Sensible or virtuous behaviour; judicious self-control
3a Controlling, directing, or regulating influence; control, mastery
3b The state of being governed; good order
3c The action or fact of governing a nation, a person, an activity, one's desires etc,; direction, rule, regulation
4   The manner in which something is governed or regulated; method of management, system of regulation. (*Oxford English Dictionary*)

Governance: competing narratives and experiences

The word *governance* in its contemporary meaning emerged in the 1970s to reflect and seek to explain the broader role of other actors and wider civil society in the work of government (Bevir, 2010). As a theory of governing (Stoker, 1998), it was widely adopted through the 1990s by international institutions and disseminated as a guide to practice through the work of the UN, OECD, World Bank and International Monetary Fund.

The use of the term governance reflects the bifurcation between a civic and an economic view of the system of governmentality. It appeared at first sight to offer a step in the democratization of the process of governing. By opening the world of hidden informal influences to a wider process of engagement, it promised to recognize the contribution and concerns of different parts of society and to create the prospect of change in the dynamics of power. It is this emancipatory form of governance that offers the prospect of minimizing domination by particular groups and interests, to give transparency to decisions, and potentially either to shift away from the function of governing as one purely of economic efficiency or at least to recognize the winners and losers of that process. This emancipatory view of governance remains in perpetual tension with its neoliberal framing in which the use of the term governance instead of government became a justification for reducing the scale and nature of government and exercising fresh control over social order and promotion of wealth through increased marketization and privatization. It was this latter form that appeared to dominate the international institutions' view of governance. I recall my former colleagues at the Department of the Environment were busy promoting the benefits of the privatization of the water industry to developing countries in the margins of the World Summit in Johannesburg in 2002. They were distinctly annoyed when Welsh First Minister Rhodri Morgan gave a radio interview on the alternative Welsh not-for-profit model.

When I first worked under the Thatcher government, some formal societal partnership vehicles continued from the post-war era. I think particularly of the National Economic Development Council (familiarly termed Neddy) which was set up under the Conservative Macmillan government in 1962 to bring together organized labour and business representatives. The one meeting I attended of the Council, chaired by my former Secretary of State, Lord Ridley, was a desultory affair late in the Thatcher government where it was clearly going through the motions of joint working. The Council was abolished in 1992 under the subsequent John Major government – a last institutional example of the consensual welfare politics of the post-war era in the UK.

Decentralization: democratization or small government?

In the early 1990s new innovations with promise of democratizing governance came into fashion, again prompted by advocacy from international economic institutions. These were forms of decentralization and devolution of power from central government. While advocated in the name of administrative responsiveness and consonant with increased democratic accountability, they can again be viewed through a neoliberal lens as a push for 'small government', a 'hollowing out' later encapsulated in the UK by the Cameron government's push for a particular form of 'localism' and 'Big Society' (2010–16). Decentralization (or, more accurately, administrative deconcentration) was embraced institutionally in the UK with the creation of the new English regional Government Offices in 1994. Subsequently the UK pursued political devolution to newly established parliaments in the constituent countries of Scotland and Wales and in Northern Ireland. In England, initial limited devolution to London and its mayor was followed by transfers of authority and budgets to directly elected mayors in several metropolitan regions.

Taking the promise of the stated motivation for the UK's decentralization at its face value, however naïvely, I pursued both formal and informal partnering and participation across my work as Environment and Transport Director in the Government Office for the South-West and in my early focus as Head of Policy for the new Welsh Government. In both the regional offices and in Wales, the opportunity provided for the bureaucracy was to create more responsive, open administration, attuned to local needs and opportunities, and to explore the potential of governance for sustainable development through a more joined-up spatial approach across the differing departmental interests.

Participative governance: subtly differing narratives

I arrived in the Government Office for the South-West fresh from working with London-based interest, academic and professional groups on the environmental dimensions of transport, and the possibility of adopting more sustainable approaches. In the South-West region, the controversial Batheaston bypass had recently been completed outside the World Heritage site of Bath. There were plans for a new elevated bypass for Salisbury which would have cut across the meadows featured in Constable's painting of the cathedral, and pressure to upgrade the road towards Cornwall to motorway quality. There seemed an opportunity here for our Office to bring people together to agree new approaches and to set out a transport policy both from and for the region. Tapping into my networks and the formal government and representative structures for transport in the South-West, my team organized a conference. I congratulated myself on my commitment to engagement. On the day, to my surprise, protestors were assembled on the roof of the building, abseiling with banners protesting road schemes. My understanding of interest networks and representative bodies had left important voices out. It was a reminder that the power of convening – who gets to be in the room – is one of the strongest controlling tools of governance and needs constant reflection if it is to avoid reproducing existing power structures. We did eventually produce a policy statement – Foucault would be proud – agreed by the main groups and presented to the Transport Minister, but it was a useful lesson on the complexity of trying genuinely to co-produce a policy position with wide interests of differing formal status.

The language describing forms of participation at this time was sometimes used interchangeably but had widely different implications. The voluntary sector suddenly became non-governmental organizations (NGOs) and lumped in with business and other representation. The participative call of the term governance came to be reflected in the widespread use of the term 'stakeholder', adopted by the UN for its arrangements. This term came to favour established organized groups and business interests. The formal UN stakeholder groups recognized in the Rio Declaration and adopted by the UN Conference on Sustainable Development reflected those at the original Rio table. We found, when establishing the network of regional governments for sustainable development (with the help of the aptly named NGO 'Stakeholder Forum for our Common Future'), that this was a closed list, albeit that we eventually achieved UN accreditation. Carl Death has taken a revealing Foucauldian look at governmentality of the UN process (Death, 2010).

Stakeholder neatly shifts the focus from emancipatory terms like inclusion, rights and social justice to become an engagement of those who have a vested interest in an issue or activity. These are typically those with financial interest and resources to engage. It can place very different interests and rights on the same level – diminishing less powerful voices and specific rights and protections.

Participation is not just a question of who is in the room but who is heard. Participative governance demands an active shaping of process and rules of engagement if it is to minimize domination. This is a long way from the traditional and often legally required formal consultation with interested parties, a tradition which can be traced back to concerns over impacts of decisions on property rights. The modernized version of this is the written policy consultation where the policy statement is sent out, or more often put online, for critique, using a pro forma which poses specific questions based on the statement text. This is then followed by a report recording in summary the responses received and how they have been reflected in a final text. At its worst, such consultation is a process of legal legitimation rather than participation and voice.

Steering not rowing: delivery relationships

Governance is associated with the mantra that government should be 'steering not rowing'. The term was used by E.S. Savas in his unequivocally titled book *Privatization: The Key to Better Government* (Savas, 1988). Drawing on a play on words worthy of a Platonic dialogue, he invoked the etymological Greek root of governing as steering (even though it had attained its modern use as governing by the Roman period – *gubernator* or governor). Despite strong links to arguments about efficiency through privatization, the aphorism again skirts the edges of control or democratization. In one respect the idea can be an acknowledgement of the legitimacy of the role of the state in setting the boundaries, rules and objectives for inclusive governance as a whole – something that would be consonant with civic republicanism. At the other end of the interpretative spectrum, it can be a call for government to absent itself from service delivery and from interventions, especially in the context of welfare provision, and to pursue widespread marketization, deregulation and privatization of public services.

Governance as steering is often described academically as operating through a combination or choice of hierarchies (the Weberian model), networks (associated with New Public Governance (Osborne, 2010)) or markets (New Public Management). Hierarchies rely on formal authority provided by state structures. Networks use the formal or informal influences of connections between state and non-state entities or groupings. The market gives steers through the price signal and in contractual terms agreed with government. All of these are ultimately strongly influenced by actions of government: government's relationship with different external networks; government's role in setting the nature of the market; and the way government exercises formal authority. This is not state retreat so much as state reconfiguration to sustain its *biopouvoir*.

For the first new Welsh Government after the devolution of powers to Wales, 'working in partnership' with civil society was the alternative mantra of governance. Devolution in Wales was viewed by its advocates as an opportunity to provide democratic voice in a country which had been administered largely through a series of central government quangos (Osmond, 1998). Many of the early Cabinet also brought extensive experience in the voluntary sector or local government. Building on legal provisions in the Government of Wales Act 1998 for formal partnerships with the voluntary sector, local government and business/labour, all activities came to be described through a loose narrative of partnering.

My team commissioned research from Cardiff University in 2002 to see how well the partnership idea was being followed through. The research suggested that the implementation of the approach had lacked clarity about whether it was aimed at efficiency and new ways of funding activity (on the Whitehall model) or partnering and including different voices (on the Welsh model). This was reflected in the specification of partnership-based activities, such as the flagship local regeneration programme, Communities First, where the focus on control and attracting funding sat oddly with the partnership aims of inclusion and joining up (Entwistle et al, 2007). There was a careless falling back in the bureaucratic design towards practices of hierarchical control and financial tests which meant the programmes never had a chance to realize their partnering aspirations.

Wales and attempted resistance to governance narratives

The Welsh Government sought to set itself apart from the governance narratives of a managerialist neoliberalism dominating the Whitehall government in a revealing exercise in 'counter-conduct'. In a speech in 2002, dubbed the 'clear red water' speech, Welsh Labour First Minister Rhodri Morgan (2000–9) set out an alternative approach to the Labour government in London (Davies and Williams, 2009): 'Government can and must be a catalyst for change and a force for good in society. Although to a Welsh audience this may sound simple stuff, it is a certainly an idea which would be contested elsewhere.' The contrast in approach was initially seen in the introduction of additional social policy measures, most notably the abolition of prescription charges in 2007. Structurally it was reflected in the merger into the Welsh executive of the inherited arm's-length economic agencies (Welsh Development Agency, Wales Tourist Board and ELWa [Education and Learning Wales]) in the 2006 'bonfire of the quangos'. In the Welsh Government's approach to governing, it was reflected in a shift away from the metrics of control. This included the ending of school league tables and a collaborative not competitive approach to delivering citizen- (not consumer-) facing services with local government and other public bodies in Wales ('Making the Connections' (WG, 2004a)). Intellectually, the approach was also pursued in experiments in adopting Scandinavian thinking in early years education and public health, and in the first Wales Spatial Plan (WG, 2004b) with its collaborative approach to investment decisions and strategic land use planning. The following years, however, demonstrated how difficult it would be to hold the line against the dominant framing of governance as short-term control and marketization.

Choice or voice?

The Welsh Government pushed back on the New Public Management mantra of providing choice in services, a push for privatization based in economic rational choice theory. Wales advocated voice, not choice, in its approach to public services. Within direct service provision to individuals, beginning with health and social services, the Welsh Government embraced the concept of co-production of care between the individual and the professional provider

Even in the search for voice, the emancipatory quality of the idea of co-design or co-production of care can become confused and ambiguous in implementation. The alternate classical economic focus on problems being the fault of the individual means voice blended into a public health call for individuals to take more responsibility for their own health. The intended empowerment offered by voice thus shifted easily to moving responsibility to those least able structurally to act, or, as First Minister Rhodri Morgan once chided me when I was exploring issues of worklessness in Wales: "Don't blame the poor for being poor."

Contracting out and public–private partnerships

Despite the Welsh Government's antipathy to the neoliberal governance narrative, UK manifestations such as the commissioning of health and social care services from third parties or across internal markets were widely embedded across Welsh public services by the time of its creation. The Welsh Government formally eschewed public–private partnerships for the provision and operation of its own public services such as health care, but the legal absence of significant borrowing powers for the Welsh Government forced applications of various forms of private finance for other infrastructure. Within my own departmental responsibilities, this included supporting local government consortia to commission the provision of new municipal recycling facilities through the award of guaranteed multi-annual contracts with private suppliers.

Performance management, targetry and league tables

Wales also found itself introducing performance targets for public bodies under media and political pressure of standardization, especially in health and social care, driven by the narrative of the 'postcode lottery' for services. This closely tracked the peak period of New Public Management's rise to becoming the main narrative test of effective and efficient governance in the UK. This period culminated in amendment to the 2008 Welsh experiment in a Scandinavian approach to early years education based on experiential learning and play – the Foundation phase curriculum. In the face of poor Welsh results in the international PISA (OECD Program for International Student Assessment) educational attainment rankings, a National Literacy and Numeracy Framework was introduced in 2013 and school performance league tables were reintroduced in 2015. This partial volte-face demonstrated the controlling power of league tables and a targetry culture. The comparative exam performance rankings prompted change even though they were not testing the purpose of the educational changes, focused as they were on personal and social development, and empowering teachers to teach creatively (Auld and Morris, 2016).

Continuing pressure for direct performance management also put strains on the collaborative performance model with local government. The performance of local government services came to dominate the political agenda, culminating in the 2013–14 Welsh Government appointed Williams Commission (WG, 2014), which advocated legal change in local government structure on the basis of the perceived inadequate size of many authorities to meet their responsibilities. Structural change for efficiency also came to dominate education and health provision as small rural schools and hospitals were progressively consolidated into larger units at the expense of their local community value.

Purpose of governance: it's the economy stupid

If governance as a term proved not to be as emancipatory as I had thought, how is this most clearly reflected? As Foucault identified, the ultimate purpose and test of governance remains political economy, expressed in the core narrative of an efficient state, the need for continued 'growth' in the simplistic metrics of GVA or GDP and the associated use of land, people and resources to support it. The prime narrative of contemporary western governance is the notion of economic efficiency rather than social justice and inclusion. Growth alone is presented as the means to provide for livelihoods and to be able to afford investment in 'nice to have' social or environmental protections.

One of the features of government and in turn governance since the early 1930s depression has been the extent to which it has become increasingly and overtly focused on the language of economy, in its modern sense of the operation of the system of commercial exchange, and the arguments of economic theorists. Not since the 18th-century debates of free trade versus protectionism has economics been so central to politics. There is nothing overtly about 'the economy' in the 1900 British Conservative or Liberal manifestos: they focus on foreign policy and aspects of social or political reform. Indeed, in the early part of the 20th century, economy still had the predominant meaning of efficient spending as used in the Independent Liberal manifesto of 1922. The political language of the 1920s/1930s crash is about specific aspects of economic management – currency devaluation, dumping and tariffs. Full or high employment and maintaining the balance of payments are the terms of the main 1945 UK manifestos. But through the 20th century, with the move from protectionist to free trade approaches and the rise and fall of Keynesian economics, the health of the economy itself came to replace other expressions of the main purpose of the state. This was accompanied by a shift in academic dominance, as the sociology of welfarism and the history of great nations was overtaken by the economists as the high priests of public policy and media reporting. A brief review of articles in the *New York Times* (Wolfers, 2015) shows economists overtaking historians in the 1930s as the most cited, with peaks matching economic downturns from the 1960s onwards. It also points to the dominance of economists across public policy fields in the Congressional record since 1989, in contrast to the weak showing of sociology, even in social policy concerns.

The 'jobs and growth' narrative adopted across Europe (including Wales) after the 2008 banking crisis – and indeed the 'green recovery' narratives that have followed the COVID-19 pandemic have marked a global shift towards the primacy of the economic purpose of governance. This highlights technological and material progress, the importance of physical infrastructure for development ('productive investment') and the continued pursuit of international competitiveness on the modern model established by Michael Porter (Porter, 1998). One might neatly map these narratives on to their 19th-century economic equivalents of scientific and industrial progress, the spread of 'civilization' through empire and commerce, and mercantilist views of international trade competition.

Former Welsh First Minister Carwyn Jones called on the jobs and growth rationale when quizzed by the media about the lack of progress on key sustainable development issues during his term of office (2009–18), despite the major legislative changes undertaken in Wales: "after 2008 and the crash that happened there, climate change started to go down the agenda across the world. People were more interested in the need to prop up our economies, making sure people have money in their pockets and are secure" (BBC Wales, 23 May 2021).

Governance as domination

Neoliberalism has taken the classical theory of the operation of an effective market and the notion of rational economic man and used it to justify a particular form of politics and governance. It has turned its back on the civic republican ideal of dialogue and checks and balances. It sees governance as the enabler rather than a regulator of partisan competition between different interests as part of an unbridled 'competitive utility maximisation' (Cameron, 2018). It is comfortable with the political power wielded by economic actors, and it reinforces, or at best ignores, the structural barriers faced by many in society (Smith, 2012). This has further strengthened the bureaucratic focus on economic and managerialist tools and pulled governance further away from an inclusive and emancipatory conception, laying the foundations for the current loss of faith in institutions and democracy itself.

The dominant language of this governance is not derived from abstract ethical values but is based in classical economists' utilitarian goal of maximizing total benefit. The best way for government to do this under the classical liberal view is not to exercise controls to prevent one person or group from dominating others, but rather to guarantee the minimization of interference in individuals' lives – so that individuals can be free to express their competing desires and to act as personal benefit-maximizing economic agents. It equates successful governance with maximizing the expression of individual desires and views that as the test of success, even if the distribution of the outcomes of those desires benefits the few and disbenefits the many.

An underpinning narrative of the economic domination of governance is the identification of the purpose and meaning of life as the individual possession of wealth and the taking of rational judgements to get there – J.S. Mill's *homo economicus* (Mill, 1965). The pressure to act as a consumer and to define oneself through one's consumption is a prevalent feature of capitalist economies: from the near patriotic duty to buy new goods to promote the economy, through conscious built-in obsolescence of products, to easy availability of debt financing, to promoting ownership over the often more sensible rental or lease. Advertising intentionally promotes these values and is largely unregulated in so doing. The governance of financial and economic systems is intricately linked with the continuation of these same practices to sustain existing regimes of capital accumulation. One thinks currently of the unquestioned focus on controlling inflation as the principal measure of the economy, a focus which largely benefits those who hold debt over those in debt, or the emphasis on controlling state debt through cuts in public service rather than tax raising, a combination which benefits those most able in society, or the promotion of mega land use developments and reclamations to the benefit of big, often internationally mobile, investors. These are all choices, not truths, but present governmentality does not support tools or narratives that readily allow the limits of our regime of truth to be explored or other courses and voices to be heard.

Governance, while still deeply contested as a concept, remains an elite and technocratic process of societal steering that seeks to instruct and shape more than engage. Governance still controls and orders society principally in the promotion of national economic development and forms of social order. The disciplines applied to create this order (in Foucault's terms) vary from direct state oppression and instruments of security to the subtler structures which control the milieu and discipline behaviour – the media, employment law, health care and welfare provision, land use controls and the financial system. The question is whether such governance as new forms of domination for economic purpose is likely to serve democracies well in our post-industrial, post-modern age, where the existential threats and challenges are so very different.

Sustainable development and governmentality

As with governance, the concept of sustainable development emerged in the turbulent period of the 1960s and 1970s, as the counterculture movement challenged post-war orthodoxies about growth and development, and as the political zeitgeist perceived the economic promises of the post-war era in the democratic west to be fading. Sustainable development was one of the competing concepts for change that emerged at that time. Its roots lay in addressing concerns about the environmental impacts of modern economic development and the differential social impacts of development, particularly in a context where the Global South was emerging as a voice in international affairs.

The idea of environment in its modern sense came into currency in the early 1960s. In 1962 Rachel Carson's *Silent Spring* and Bob Dylan's *A Hard Rain's A Gonna Fall* captured for that generation the risks posed to environmental health from modernist technologies (particularly nuclear power and testing, industrial farming and pesticides, such as DDT, and widespread adoption of novel industrial chemicals, such as PCBs) and the impact of the overuse of natural resources on planetary ecology. By the late 1960s, environment was a term of art for both civil society and public policy. The first Earth Day was held in the spring of 1970. The US National Environmental Policy Act became law in 1968, followed by the creation of the US Environmental Protection Agency in 1970 and a raft of founding legislation on water and species protection. There was mounting public concern about the health of the 'environment' in its modern sense, and its increasing degradation. This was reinforced by the understanding brought by the environmental justice movement as to the unequal distribution of harmful processes to poor and majority ethnic communities in the United States, and its corollary in international development which was tragically demonstrated by the huge loss of life and injury in the 1984 Bhopal disaster.

My first job as a bureaucrat was in the UK Department of the Environment, itself founded in 1970. My first workplace – the long-demolished Environment and Transport Department building on 2 Marsham Street in Westminster – had a plaque in the entrance foyer commemorating the United Nations Conference on the Human Environment of 1972. This appeared there as if in vindication of the establishment of the first UK Department of the Environment just two years previously. It was a department in which the natural and human environments jostled across competing environmental, planning, housing, transport and local government responsibilities. That first 1972 version of an 'Earth Summit' resulted in the Stockholm Declaration which set 26 principles for governing environment and development. It also led to the establishment of the United Nations Environment Programme.

Sustainable development, as a concept, built on the impact of the Report of the Club of Rome, *Limits to Growth* (Meadows, 1972), which suggested that global population and pollution would increasingly exceed earth's capacity to sustain them. It also reflected the 1980 Report of the Independent

Commission on International Development Issues, *North-South: A Programme for Survival* (or the Brandt Report) (Brandt, 1980), which called for radical (and largely unadopted) reforms, including of international finance and trade, in order to address international inequalities.

Sustainable development was formally established in international public policy 15 years after the Stockholm Declaration by the report of the World Commission on Environment and Development, commonly referred to as the Brundtland Report (WCED, 1987). It was this report which came before us as I began my career in public service. My time in Whitehall corresponded with the introduction of Integrated Pollution Control from 1990, the production of the first UK Environment White Paper 'This Common Inheritance' (UK Government, 1990) and the start of what became in 1996 the England and Wales Environment Agency. 1992 also saw our participation in the Earth Summit in Rio where the concept of sustainable development was adopted by the international community, with commitments to conventions on climate change, biodiversity and desertification.

Today it is the Brundtland ethical mantra – 'meeting the needs of the present without compromising the ability of future generations to meet their own needs' – which is the most often cited element of the report, but the report sets out a much richer narrative in its introductory text. This introduction presents a much more radical agenda than the one my team had developed in 1990 for the first UK Environment White Paper. This radical imaginary has largely become tamed in its public policy expressions to a modified version of 'business as usual'. Yet, despite co-option by conventional forces and models of intervention, the sustainable development imaginary still offers a powerful disruptive alternative view (Baker, 2007).

The Brundtland introductory narrative offers a clear alternative stance to the global politics of the late 1980s. It calls for a return to multilateralism, common endeavour, new norms, the importance of economic and social justice globally, and bringing consumption within the earth's means. It presents the concept of sustainable development as a new global ethic, replacing what it terms 'old approaches' to maintaining social and ecological stability. This new approach is based in reflecting the interconnectedness of economic, social and environmental challenges. It talks of righting an economic system that increases rather than decreases inequality, tackling causes rather than treating environmental symptoms and changing international law and institutional missions. It sees sustainable development as a journey to be taken together, rather than a charted course to be followed, and calls on businesses, educators and wider society to engage with the journey. It calls for a human right to an environment adequate for health and well-being. In short, Brundtland uses language of fundamental socio-economic transformations.

These messages were embraced in the subsequent work by the UN Commission of Sustainable Development (1992–2013) with a focus on inter- and intra-generational equity as a basis for global action, delivered through the guiding concept of shared but differentiated international responsibilities. The process established a new set of participative mechanisms, incorporated in the declaration following the first Rio Earth Summit in 1992 (UNCED, 1992), with its commitment to transparency and public participation and access to justice as preconditions for achieving sustainable development. This spawned a range of initial activity such as Local Agenda 21 with its mantra of 'think global, act local' and led to the international adoption of the Aarhus Convention on rights of access to environmental information (UNECE, 1998).

Sustainable development remains a contested concept. In public policy it is easily adjectivalized into weaker or distorted forms – I was surprised in arriving at the Government Office for the South-West in 1995, for example, that the new Offices for the Regions had a guiding mission which included 'sustainable *economic* development'. The question of how the social, environmental and economic aspects of sustainable development should interact dominated thinking in my early career, where David Pearce worked as an advisor alongside our Environment White Paper team, fresh from his 1989 Blueprint for a Green Economy (Pearce et al, 1989) advocating costing the environment and using taxation to deal with externalities. The environmental economics conception of sustainable development, as presented in the 'three pillars' model of sustaining environmental, social and economic capital, allows for human capital to replace natural capital. The idea of weak sustainability, as it is termed, where everything is exchangeable, features heavily in public policy. It supports the continuing use of mitigation and offsetting of environmental impacts rather than avoidance. It can also be seen in the frequent public policy use of the term 'balancing' when describing action on the three capitals instead of a more aspirational 'optimizing'. Strong sustainability, where natural capital is viewed as ethically separate and an underpinning factor of the other capitals, continues to inform work by environmental NGOs and academic understanding of the interaction of socio-ecological systems including the difference between spending the flows of benefits to society and making permanent reductions in environmental stock (Ang and Passel, 2012).

Relevant to the theme of non-domination, Amartya Sen has aligned the concept of development with ideas of non-domination in socio-economic systems in his work *Development as Freedom* (Sen, 1999). Here he presents the goal of development as the ability for all to enjoy *interconnected* freedoms: from oppression, of opportunity and from poverty.

The term sustainability is often used interchangeably for sustainable development or as a term in itself without clear definition. While sustainability strictly describes a condition rather than a means, it is often presented as a stronger term than sustainable development and is associated with strong sustainability or an ecological approach in which the idea of development itself may be challenged. In the past ten years sustainable development sometimes feels to have been eclipsed as a guiding idea in academia by the notion of the Anthropocene with its call for action based on the extent to which human systems have come to dominate natural ones (McNeill, 2014). In politics, it is the narratives of climate change and low carbon economy that have seemingly taken the space occupied in the 1990s by sustainable development. Sustainable development, however, by focusing on the essential interactions of the social, environmental and economic, and directly embracing issues of justice and equity, is both more comprehensive and presents richer implications for governance.

My chosen field of work put together the two heavily contested terms of governance and sustainable development in a challenging and often confusing cocktail. For clarity, I was drawn to the Brundtland Report's introduction for its expressions of the change needed in governance and the implications for bureaucratic endeavour.

The Brundtland Report makes the express call to address the drivers of unsustainability rather than mitigating their impacts, and for this to be reflected throughout public and private institutions. The 'new ethic' stressed the need in governance:

- to reflect the *inherent interrelationship* between social, economic and environmental concerns;
- to acknowledge that pathways to change are *uncertain*;
- for *transformational* societal change; and
- for *societal dialogue* to gain commitment and help design necessary changes.

This is an ecological and civic understanding of governance based in democratic dialogue and institutional change.

In institutional terms, the report specifically pointed to the structural problem of public agencies which promoted unsustainable development not being responsible for addressing the environmental and social consequences of their actions. It also advocated strengthening the then relatively new environmental agencies and departments.

Elsewhere in the Brundtland Report, its sectoral chapters adopt a more conventional language of managing change. This has come to be associated with a less systemic and transformatory approach to governance, one that talks of sectoral transitions.

The Earth System Governance Project has specified three forms of governance approaches in relation to sustainable development (Earth Systems Governance Project, 2018). Firstly, there is the idea of governance *for* sustainable development, that is governance to enable transformational socio-economic change necessary for sustainability. The second is transformation *in* governance to reflect sustainable development, and the third is governance *of* sustainable development, which is focused on the delivery or management of specific sustainability transitions, using existing governance practice and relations in pursuit of targeted environmental outcomes, such as a reduction in greenhouse gas emissions. This distinction is a useful one, whether or not one wishes to embrace Earth System Governance's focus on replacing economic efficiency with ecological efficiency as the new primary goal of governance. Governance *for* closely reflects the Brundtland Report's call for a new global ethic and offers a new purpose for governance. Governance *of* sustainable development is about managed sectoral change, much of which is set out in the specific topic chapters of the Brundtland Report. With my focus on the role of public bureaucracy, I seek to explore the transformational change *in* governance that I argue is a necessary part of the ability to enable transformational change *for* sustainable development.

Governing for *sustainable development: socio-ecological transformation*

The bulk of academic focus on the implications of sustainable development for governance has sought to flesh out the details of the original call of the Brundtland Report. This work has emphasized the need for long-term 'societal self-steering' to achieve deep transformations (Meadowcroft, 2007). Such transformations are needed across multiple systems and are dynamic and interactive (Patterson et al, 2017). Social, economic, cultural and environmental issues involve complex interconnected systems which can no longer be pursued in isolation without regard to wider consequences (Holling, 2001). The complexity of these systems and their interconnections cannot be managed or controlled in the traditional bureaucratic sense, nor can they be rationalized away or described in traditional economic approaches but instead they need to be explored and revealed by effective participative and deliberative democracy (Dryzek and Pickering, 2019). In this way decision-making may begin to match natural systems in becoming reflexive or adaptive (Folke et al, 2005) and to engage with local and non-specialist knowledge and understandings to address the considerable uncertainty regarding the results of interventions (Voß and Bornemann, 2011).

The needs of participation, systems-understanding and reflexivity leads to an emphasis on place-based action that can better understand and identify the connections between social, economic and environmental impacts (Baker and Durance, 2018). Place-based governance can reflect the different scales at which interacting systems can be considered together and optimized (Ostrom, 2010) and provide the basis for effective local collective management (Ostrom, 2009).

Unhelpfully, sustainability governance literature often uses the terms transitions and transformation interchangeably. While not an argument to deal with in depth here, I distinguish transformatory change as one which leads to a new understanding and dynamic system functioning. This is not a simple transition from one fixed state to the next. It is governing *for* that seeks to change the purpose of governance in a way that fundamentally challenges existing power relationships and norms. In Foucault's terms, this means reshaping the drivers shaping the milieu which determines what is possible. It is this form of transformative governance which was demanded in the introduction to the Brundtland Report, and which has major implications for how we organize governance and the existing tools of bureaucratic life.

John Barry (Barry, 2008) has pointed out the untapped synergy between civic republicanism and the transformational aspirations of green politics. In *The Green State*, Robyn Eckersley (Eckersley, 2004) presents a dissection of the established theories of governance and the state, the barriers they present to embracing ecological imperatives and the potential for change. Based in critical theory and its focus on emancipation from domination, she extends the civic republican notion of non-domination and dialogue to include the non-human world and posits a post-liberal democratic state that has structures which can serve to address rather than hide the pressing ecological concerns. *Ecological Governance* (Jennings, 2016) likewise dissects the problems of inherited narratives of the purpose of governance and their poor fit with the challenges of the Anthropocene. Rather than reaching to civic republicanism, he turns to reconceiving social contract theory, especially looking to Rousseau, to propose a new ecological ethic for governance based in the desire for transcendent rather than rational values. As with Barry and Eckersley this approach includes aspects of discursive democracy and constitutionalism in its foundation.

While academic focus has filled in some of the gaps in the practical forms of change in governance that could reflect the Brundtland call, there has been least work undertaken on how this repurposing of governance needs to be reflected in transformation in the practice of bureaucracy. The emphasis here to date has largely been on international institutions and on forms of public engagement and representation, especially legal forms of deliberative or discursive governance which could enable societal self-steering. Little linkage has been made between transformation for sustainable development and critical work in the field of public administration such as that of New Public Service (Denhardt and Denhardt, 2007), which has placed a similar emphasis on civic dialogue, or to related writing on the nature and limitations of existing approaches to public administration reform (Christensen and Lægreid, 2007). The main focus of this book is to fill this gap by considering how continuing to work with existing technologies of power based on other aims and values constitutes a barrier to enabling the form of transformatory outcomes called for in the Brundtland ethic, and to begin to paint a picture of how, and with what effect, this practice could change.

Governance of sustainable development

The main focus of policy and bureaucratic practice to date has not been on the transformational prospect of governing *for* sustainable development but has pursued governance *of* sustainable development. Here writing focuses on governing the delivery of specific goals or sectoral changes and seeking economic and technical efficiencies. This can overlap with the concept of management of transitions, drawing on the Dutch planning tradition (Loorbach, 2007). Governance *of* employs a largely conventional set of institutional relationships, processes and problem-framing. It retains existing systems and values of controlling governmentality such as those for the development and management of the use of land and the mitigation of pollution. It frames sustainable development as a series of discrete challenges with separate delivery mechanisms and targets and is focused on sectoral action.

Governance *of* has largely co-opted the radical concept of sustainable development from being 'a new global ethic' to pursuing existing dominant forms and narratives of governance. This governance *of* has utilized conventional ideas and tools of modern governance. Governance *of* continues to apply the language of economic efficiency and management rather than of interconnected systems and transformations.

Governance *of* uses existing technologies of power. Its toolkit applies existing modes such as technocratic managerialism, market measures, behavioural instruments, setting of goals and targets and use of economic appraisals. It focuses effort on engaging representatives of interest groups rather than wider society. Emphasis is placed on the scope for technical solutions which minimize the need for socio-economic change. Governance *of* is perhaps best captured in the concept dubbed 'ecological modernisation' (Baker, 2007). This reinforces the traditional governance goal of economic efficiency and the market economy, in promoting the idea that it will be new industries, responding to changing consumer and market conditions, which can drive reductions in resource use or pollutant emissions. It is a conception that the system that brought us to this point of crisis can be gently steered to something very different.

Mirroring the shifts in the wider adoption of the term governance, the delivery of this version of sustainable development governance has moved to non-public sector models. The 2002 Earth Summit introduced the potentially emancipatory idea of what it termed 'Type II partnerships' – agreements involving civil society actors in addition to existing governmental responsibilities. These were welcomed as an opening up of international governing beyond governments, but the move was also criticized as a marketization of the funding and delivery of environmental action, a reduction in accountability, and a new source of imbalance between North and South (Andonova and Levy, 2003).

It is governance *of* that has been favoured more recently in international institutions such as the UN – particularly since the second Rio Summit and the resulting abandonment of the Brundtland-inspired United Nations Commission on Sustainable Development (UNCSD) process and its replacement with the High Level Political Forum – and in the EU in its adoption of ecological modernization as its policy focus. It is reflected in the UN Sustainable Development Goals, with their long list of distinct, contradictory aims, and in the processes of the Climate Change and Biodiversity Conventions. Governance *of* is typically structured as technocratic governance aligning with institutions, non-governmental actors and processes. It works with limited participation which reflects disconnected interests rather than systemic relationships. It is deterritorialized, placing little interest in place-based and co-produced engagement and delivery. It works with conventional structures of power, and it favours market-based solutions combined with governmental accountability for targeted commitments. It is a familiar, comfortable set of mechanisms and narratives for both administrators, politicians and lobbyists.

Welsh contrariness

The Welsh Government's 'counter-conduct' in governance from 2002 included attempts to make greater sense of the application of its general sustainable development duty. First Minister Rhodri Morgan attended the Johannesburg Summit and co-founded the network of regional governments for sustainable development, co-chairing the work on the Gauteng Declaration on the role of sub-national governments. He maintained lead responsibility for sustainable development until it was handed over to a new department in 2007.

The Welsh legal sustainable development schemes developed increased maturity. The first scheme was a conventional take on sustainable development as something to integrate into the way conventional policy and programmes are run. Using borrowed language from UK policy, *Learning to Live Differently* (National Assembly, 2000) stated the commitment: 'We will integrate the principles of sustainable development into our work and seek to influence others to do the same.'

The second scheme, *Starting to Live Differently* (National Assembly, 2004), has a more distinctive voice, while sharing the same basic structure and title style. It repeated the UK principles but set the aims of the new programme for government, *Wales: A Better Country*, alongside a refreshed framework of principles for sustainable development. This moved closer to the Brundtland ethic in stating that sustainable development underpins and drives (rather than being integrated with) everything the Assembly does and that wherever possible the root causes of problems should be tackled. The scheme sets out implementation through the new Wales Spatial Plan, with an emphasis on distinctive place-based responses. Unlike the first scheme it is explicit that current 'ways of living' are unsustainable.

The third scheme, *One Wales: One Planet* (WG, 2009), the first issued in the name of Welsh Assembly Government after the end of Wales' accidental experiment in a unified government and executive, incorporated its own action plan and defined what it meant by sustainable development:

> Sustainable development means enhancing the economic, social and environmental wellbeing of people and communities, achieving a better quality of life for our own and future generations, in ways which promote social justice and equality of opportunity; and which enhance the natural and cultural environment and respect its limits – using only our fair share of the earth's resources and sustaining our cultural legacy. Sustainable development is the process by which we reach the goal of sustainability.

Goals included achieving an economy that is able to develop while stabilizing, then reducing, its use of natural resources and reducing its contribution to climate change, and that citizens of all ages and backgrounds are empowered to determine their own lives, shape their communities and achieve their full potential, and that sustainable development was the central organizing principle for governance. Together, these pushed closer to a governance *for* model and the Brundtland ethic.

The statutory reviews of the respective schemes make for salutary reading. Each review points to incremental progress and specific positive initiatives – most notably the novel policy appraisal process as an early attempt to join up policy and programmes, and specific resource efficiency steps, such as the introduction of charges for single-use bags. Overall, however, the reviews suggest a failure to shift the existing centre ground of the narratives and goals of government towards the delivery of sustainable development. The lack of progress demonstrated that the simple commitment to change was not enough. Indeed, change required not only a clearer sense of what constituted sustainable development as a guiding idea (as largely achieved in the third scheme) but also, as with the other Welsh attempts at differentiation highlighted earlier in this chapter, they required a deeper understanding of the corresponding change needed to address the barriers posed by competing governance and bureaucratic narratives, priorities and practice. It was the realization of the importance of addressing in detail the nature of such barriers that led to the final scheme evolving into a political proposal for fresh legislation. This was to become the Well-being of Future Generations (Wales) Act 2015.

The democratic impasse

Academically, the lack of fundamental reorientation of governance to achieve progress towards sustainable development has been termed a democratic impasse (Meadowcroft et al, 2012). The impasse had been ascribed to many core issues. There is the partisan 'competitive democracy' model which Lafferty (Lafferty, 2012) sees (just as does civic republicanism) as inimical to producing the deep debate and consensus needed for structural change and long-term thinking. There are the voters themselves, wedded, as Blühdorn has suggested, to the politics of unsustainability (Blühdorn and Welsh, 2008). Here, we are individually and collectively seen as too committed to the drivers of unsustainability – consumption, private property and motorized travel – to wish to see substantive change. There is the call for non-growth economics (Jackson, 2009) or 'a-growth' politics (Bergh, 2011) in the face of the fundamental pact between liberal democracy and capitalism which drives short-termism and the push for constant growth in consumption and development of land. There is the conscious distancing and disconnect in modern life between the natural and the human, or between consumption and its consequences, with calls for the common good to be found in a new ecological integrity (Baker, 2012). There are the broad 'vested interests' in the status quo – an issue which many of my academic colleagues cited first when I asked them informally about barriers to governing for sustainable development (showing a perhaps surprising belief in rational self-interest!).

From a Foucauldian perspective, we can suggest that the present impasse is all these things because, at heart, these can all be seen as different aspects of the self-reproduction of the entire governance system. It is a reproduction sustained by narratives that tap into and reinforce deeply embedded values, constrained by the overall milieu established and maintained by territorial organization and socio-economic pressures, and regulated by the inherited practices of bureaucracy. It is the historically-rooted model for sustaining an industrial society. It is the systemic mismatch between the Brundtland ethic and existing narratives and structures of governance and their bureaucratic technologies of power that lies at the heart of the impasse.

Using Foucault's characteristics of power, the approach of governance *of* sustainable development pursues existing aims and uses existing forms of control. It relies heavily on knowledge-power in its technocracy and managerialism. In pursuing market measures and sectoral transitions, it sees political economy as its primary form of knowledge. In seeking behavioural or technical rather than structural change, it maintains the main systems of control, without impacting on territorial organization or existing forms of domination. Its narratives treat nature as subservient to human needs and desires and to the dominant economic system. This has served to reinforce the persistence of unsustainability by constraining practices, narratives and in turn possibilities. At its worst, this creates a pretence of commitment to sustainability while changing none of the underlying drivers.

Taking Foucault's conceptions of the role of knowledge-power, biopower and territory in shaping existing governance, and taking 'minimization of domination' as an ideal, suggests that governance *of* – the present mechanics and matrices for the delivery of specific aspects of sustainable development – is *prima facie* reproductive of existing practice, values and outcomes. The concept of governing *for*, seen through the same lens, creates the prospect for the transformational change envisaged in Brundtland's 'new global ethic'. This approach challenges core elements *in* current governance and bureaucratic practice. Notably it requires acceptance of an ecological rather than a mechanistic analogy for how governance should work, one that can embrace non-conventional forms of knowledge, uncertainty, complex interactions and societal self-steering. These strike at the heart of the use of technologies of knowledge-power and territory, the technocracies that are key in Foucault's writing to establishing and sustaining modern regimes of truth. The roots of this conflict in the exercise of knowledge-power provides an appropriate bridge into discussion in the following chapter of the specific constraining role played by bureaucracy and its practice, and also connects with the societal disaffection that feeds the politics of post-truth.

3

Bureaucratic practice and governmentality

> The Corporation is civil society's attempt to become state; but the bureaucracy is the state which has really made itself into civil society.
>
> Karl Marx

Memories

As a final year student looking for a job, I was first attracted to the UK civil service by the intellectual environment and variety of roles it offered. With a certain innocence, I also had the sense of the service as operating systems which arbitrated impartially between differing societal interests in pursuit of the wider public interest. This was how I picked my initial department and first post – the Department of the Environment, working in the Planning: Land Use Policy division.

Day one as a fast-stream new entrant was an introduction to hierarchy and differentiation. I was first assigned a desk, to receive the comment from my new co-workers, only half in jest, that it had two too many drawers for my grade. There was also some humour about entitlements to a size of carpet or of room. I then was sent to collect my office supplies and was asked at the supplies room whether I was worthy of a green administrative tray, set aside for those of us who worked on policy, or a grey executive tray set aside for those who dealt with process. This distinction for civil servants dated back to Gladstone's time as Chancellor of the Exchequer under Queen Victoria, as the 'footing best calculated for the efficient discharge of their important functions according to the actual circumstances of the present time' and was still very much alive and well. The history of the civil service cast a long shadow. When I came to attend the then UK Civil Service College, the main buildings on the site were named after Northcote and Trevelyan – the 19th-century authors of the Gladstonian Reforms.

My boss's boss and his seniors had wooden, rather than metal, furniture, including a bookcase and small allocated drinks cabinet. My Assistant Secretary memorably took me for a long lunch at the local Italian restaurant, presumably to show me the potential rewards of the life to come. Directors and above automatically appeared in the British publication of *Who's Who* and our most senior staff were awarded knighthoods shortly after their appointment. There was a faded spirit of empire about the place. It was much clearer what your grade was than your function. A fly-on-the-wall documentary made of my year of fast-stream interviews showed the persistent elitism and social bias of recruitment to the senior civil service, not so very different from Kelsall's classic 1955 account of *Higher Civil Servants in Britain* (Kelsall, 1955). I vividly recall my own surprise (and my surprise at my surprise) when I first shook hands in the mid-1990s with a Permanent Secretary who was thickset and had a firm handshake!

Our role as administrators was the production of papers – with the aim of creating policy positions or decisions (or Foucault's 'statements') and always with the inevitability of producing, in those days before ready computer storage, large paper records (or Max Weber's 'files'). When sending policy advice to ministers there was a strict requirement to copy these to those who were senior to you in the direct hierarchy – but no others unless there was a very direct interest, with their names duly recorded on the header of the paper. In my departments, the copy list was done by name in top down order of seniority, in others, like the Ministry of Defence, it was purely by job title and rank. I still have the scar from where I hit my head when wrestling with a recalcitrant photocopier trying to pull together the massive list of copies of a ministerial submission.

Our main building was set out in three separate towers connected only on two lower floors. The towers reflected the original units that had come together to form the department in the 1970s. Ministers had their own floor in the respective towers: Transport, Environment and Planning and Local Government and Housing. We were notionally together but physically (and mentally) separate. We were also a long way distant from my lived experience growing up in the industrial East Midlands. I had joined a very distinct setting.

Practice of bureaucracy and the barriers to transformation in governance

Bureaucracy, 'the power of the office', captures the idea that public policy and administrative mechanisms and norms, narratives and institutions sustain particular forms of governance. This 'practice' of governance (or '*dispositifs*' in Foucault's terms (Foucault, 2008)) sustains a set of values and outcomes through particular forms of consideration and action or inaction. Foucault's framing places an emphasis on the importance of repetition or performance of practices and of accompanying legitimizing narratives – supported by various forms of discipline and underpinned by knowledge-power. These sustain particular forms and norms of governance and dynamically create and recreate corresponding conditions or milieu.

Bureaucracy has not received positive press since it was coined as a term in mid-18th-century France, but bureaucracy matters in this discussion of the challenge of transformative efforts. The unstated assumptions of bureaucratic practice make bureaucracy its own actor in the interplay of governance. For all its focus on being apolitical, bureaucracy is not neutral but applies a set of often unstated values based chiefly in pursuing the generalized economic efficiency of the state. The unreflective application of practice or values within the different bureaucratic roles of policy professionals, project managers, specialists and operational staff, shapes how public bureaucrats variously make propositions to ministers, design responses to ministerial ideas, put in place mechanisms to deliver decisions or laws, develop policy positions and plans, undertake the day-to-day financial and operational management and provide the public interface of programmes of work. Within this system bureaucrats make choices based on both the conventions of the system and on their collective and individual sense of bureaucratic purpose and legitimacy.

Reflecting now, as an escapee from public bureaucracy, I am struck how often in my working life practice drawn from completely different perspectives – say, measures to foster participation and those to assert control – co-existed without any sense of the inherent conflict. I also experienced a high degree of careless mimetics, especially as neoliberalism became a dominant force in bureaucratic reform. Fashionable approaches – like New Public Management's insistence on targets, contracting out of services or competitive funding – were adopted as a new normal even where these seemed an odd fit with political inclination. In the absence of a coherent view of the values and purpose of bureaucracy, language and approaches borrowed from different framings of bureaucracy, governance and sustainable development serve to distort implementation and drag transformatory intent back to more conventional controls. The instruments of governance matter: 'instruments at work are not neutral devices: they produce specific effects, independently of the objective pursued (the aims ascribed to them), which structure public policy according to their own logic' (Lascoumes and Le Gales, 2007).

Genealogy of bureaucratic narratives

Taking Foucault's historical genealogical approach reminds that current truths were not always considered as such but emerged from the patterns of past narratives. Narratives draw on and reinforce old values. Underlying most of these narratives, there is male privilege and misogyny and White privilege and racial injustice. There is the dualist separation of the human and the natural worlds. There is the sense that land is only of value when developed or improved. There is seeing the rural as a failed form of urbanism that has little relevance beyond a nostalgic beauty. There is considering other cultures, languages and the arts and humanities as unproductive and irrelevant, or viewing one's own nation or people as naturally superior. This range of powerful historic narratives and values are drawn from a mishmash of competing assumptions of the nature of humankind and the purpose of life and tap into the unreflexive mind to create truisms. Such unstated viewpoints lie in shadow behind the values and practice of bureaucracy. As Douglas Torgerson (Torgerson, 2005, 99) succinctly puts it: 'What remains of old is not a method, but an aura, one that envelops the image of rationality and obscures the limits of the administrative mind.'

Western bureaucracy arose from the late 18th century alongside the acceptance of the centrality of economic performance to the well-being of the state. Sir James Steuart first set out the English-language case for orientating the state towards economic efficiency in *An Inquiry into the Principles of Political Economy* (Steuart, 1767). This favoured a self-supporting economy of reciprocal relations which would bind society together and meet everyone's material needs. Steuart advocated targeted restrictions on overseas trading to support this aim. This economic purpose of the state was honed by the classical liberal perspectives of writers such as Adam Smith (Smith, 2007) who defined the nature of an efficient state in market freedoms and the forms of government which should accompany them. This provided economic *purpose* as the legitimacy for state action and a separate and evolving set of economic legitimacy tests of the detailed *organization and practice* of the state.

The formal rise of western public bureaucracy – and its emphasis on these two expressions of economic efficiency – is strongly aligned to the rise of the application of governmentality in the nation state and colonial empires. For Foucault, this process of bureaucratization was a formative part of the move to the modern state where order and discipline creates control over populations, established through institutions and procedures of technocratic bureaucracy and the associated management of territory (Foucault, 2008). In his lectures, he traces the move from a religious legitimacy for the state's exercise of power to one based in technocracy with the aim of the promotion of the efficiency of the state. Here bureaucracy is expressly both the machinery and guardian of order of the modern state.

The nationalist tradition of bureaucracy was strongly shaped by Kammeralism in the Germanic Kingdoms. Kammeralism emerged as an academic discipline in Prussia focused on the efficient organization and operation of bureaucracy to support the wider efficiency of state. This was in part a response to the large colonial empires which provided wealth to neighbouring nations. As well as focusing on state bureaucracy, Kammeralism as an academic discipline advocated state action to maximize production and export including training for landowners to maximize output. J.H. Gottlob von Justi, an 18th-century popularizer of Kammeralism, advocated state economic success through a moderated monarchy with strong protection of property rights. He argued for abolition of guild restrictions, tax reform and the need for government interventions to promote trade and industry (Nokkala, 2009). Kammeralism has left us not only with this bureaucratic application of political economy but, more specifically, the techniques of its measurement as a core function of bureaucracy and measure of success. This includes the practice of statistics, the recording of imports and exports and the cameral – or annualized – financial accounting used by most governments. It is the Kammeralist world that Max Weber critiques in his classic writings on bureaucracy in *Wirtschaft und Gesellschaft* (Weber, 1922).

Britain drew explicitly on its imperial colonial experience in constructing its bureaucracy. The sprawling British colonialism in India, established by the East India Company, can be regarded as first large-scale western professional bureaucracy. The East India Company's administrators were termed 'writers' – reflecting the strong focus on recording and accounting in their role – and from 1809 they had their own professional training college. Given that this was a company running a country, the focus on profit, productivity and trade was absolute (Dalrymple, 2019). At the height of the opium trade with China, the company's Opium Agency employed 2,500 clerks in 100 officers to monitor production and manage contracting and loans for local poppy farmers (Bauer, 2019). Thomas Taylor Meadows, in his work *Desultory Notes on the Government and People of China and on the Chinese Language* (Meadows, 1847) popularized the idea that it was the professional hierarchical administration of China that had been a key to that country's stability and success. The nature of a professional, impartial, meritocratic public service was established by the report commissioned by the British government from senior officials Northcote and Trevelyan in 1854 on the 'Organisation of the Permanent Civil Service' (Lowe, 2011). The aims of Northcote and Trevelyan persist directly in the UK civil service code (Appendix 4), although the report's formal division of workers into executive scribes and administrative policy advisors (into which I was first recruited) has faded over more recent years. In an echo of the Chinese model, senior civil servants in the UK of a traditional style are still ironically dubbed 'mandarins'.

Formal adoption of the standing bureaucratic model in the late 19th century was widely associated with addressing concerns over corruption as well as inefficiency in the existing systems. This was especially true for the widespread patronage exercised over appointments (Theriault, 2003) and the expectation that office-holders would profit from their post (seen most clearly perhaps in the system of tax farming in France). Tackling corruption and bribery and promoting transparency and accountability in public service are still seen as an essential part of 'good governance' (and civic republicanism) and feature as specific outcomes under the UN Sustainable Development Goal 16 to: 'Promote peaceful and inclusive societies for sustainable development, provide access to justice for all and build effective, accountable and inclusive institutions at all levels.' Only the repetition of the word 'inclusive' notably separates this modern expression from the historical model.

Weber and the nature of modern bureaucracy

While an expression of its time and place in turn of the century Germany, a hundred years on, Max Weber's account (Weber, 1922, Part 3, Chapter VI) arguably remains the dominant framing of bureaucratic structures and is still influential in their critique. Like Foucault, he sees bureaucracy as an aspect of domination legitimized by narratives, in this case rule of law combined with specialist knowledge which together provided predictability of decisions. He dubbed this 'legal domination with a bureaucratic administrative staff'.

Weber sets out the necessary characteristics he sees for the operation of bureaucracy in the new industrial economy (Weber, 1978, Vol 2, Chapter XI). These are strikingly analogous to the operation of industry itself. First is the division of labour in which subjects are separated out and assigned. This characteristic is still maintained in the siloed structures and responsibilities of modern bureaucratic departments. Second is its hierarchical nature through which propriety and regularity of process is maintained, again still a feature of bureaucratic organization. Third is written documentation of decisions and processes, 'the files' which provide for a record of due process, not unlike contractual records and accounting, again a central feature of bureaucracy to this day (albeit one made more complex by electronic media). Fourth is trained expertise, which is reflected both in professional disciplines and in specialist qualifications for staff and which gives legitimacy to their decisions. This varies from country to country – some emphasize legal over other skill – but higher academic qualifications remain a prerequisite for middle and senior posts. Fifth, as a buttress against corruption, the office absorbs the officer's time completely, positions should be well paid and pensioned and not a benefice, and sixth there should be general rules as to how the office functions. Together these are intended to give the objective, dispassionate discharge of business without regard to the person that Weber sees as key to the functioning of the industrial capitalist society. Weber argued that only the formal rationality of economics and bounded responsibilities provided the predictability required for economic enterprise. In a link to our theme of the fitness of governance for changing times, Weber in *The Protestant Ethic* (Weber, 2001) sees that the rational structure of the new economy meant that 'we must be vocational men'; for we are inescapably confronted by the 'mighty cosmos of the modern economic order', which will endure 'until the last ton of fossil fuel has turned to ash' (Ringer, 2004, 217).

Weber's formative account of the practice and profession of bureaucracy with its structures and uniform rules continue to sustain the 'iron cage', or, in my translation, 'adamantine shell' (in the original German 'stahlhartes Gehäuse') (Weber, 2001) within which the bureaucrat can safely exercise bounded rationality, cushioned by her dispassionate profession and distanced from the impact of decisions. In this way decision-making is presented as a uniform mechanized process for a mechanized age. Its technical disciplines and division of functions produce an 'efficient' uniformity. It cannot by its nature see the socio-economic or ecological system as a whole or have interest in making connections outside its structural 'adamantine shell'. It is arranged according to a positivistic, analytical model and rules of political economy from which it draws its legitimacy and in which the bureaucrat is safely immured.

As Ringer suggests in his intellectual biography, Weber expressed misgivings about the implications of both capitalism and bureaucracy for its impact on society and was hostile to the notion of both a planned economy and unrestrained capitalism (Ringer, 2004, Chapter 7). Like Foucault, he saw bureaucracy as a new basis of rationality for governance, necessary in the face of a shifting moral order. Yet his description of the inescapability of bureaucratic and market rationale has become a blueprint for bureaucratic organization, rationality and purpose. Weber's account is reflected in the continued organizational structures and processes of bureaucracy which it both described and continues to legitimate as the 'proper' way to govern. This form of bureaucracy is seen as an apolitical stance because it has occupied the centre ground of political thought (Heath, 2020), but it is itself a form of ideology in equating economic efficiency with rationality. Weber chose this bureaucracy reluctantly because the only alternative he could see in post-First World War Germany was revolutionary socialism. Weber's ambivalence about bureaucracy presents in his sense of bureaucracy as a self-reinforcing, unchanging, mechanical monolith. In his vocation talks, he speaks of the importance of politics in animating bureaucracy with a more than rational (technical-economic) value. He often – and rather presciently – quoted an American worker's comment to him during a stay in the US (set in the context of the spoils system) that corrupt politicians were preferable to controlling bureaucrats (Ringer, 2004, 224).

Weber's view of what legitimizes bureaucracy (in the sense of its public acceptability) also seems ambivalent. In *Economy and Society*, his description of the model bureaucracy suggests it is the rule of law and the status of expertise that gives it legitimacy. In his talks on political vocation (Dreijmanis and Wells, 2008), where he is thinking more about government, he lists the bases of legitimacy as tradition, charismatic leadership and rule of law. He goes on to state that the ruler needs the obedience of the bureaucracy, suggesting that its chief legitimacy draws from the authority of the ruler. In *Economy and Society*, Weber also points to the importance of the ability and ethos of the bureaucrat to carry out the order of superiors as if it were his own conviction. Without this, the system falls to pieces.

The discussion of different legitimacies is important as it determines how we view the role and purpose of bureaucracy. By discussing the ethos of obeying orders, Weber links forward to the principal-agent theory of administration where the bureaucracy is simply the agent of the politician and necessarily fails to understand and fully reflect what is intended (Waterman and Meier, 1998). This has in turn fostered a tendency to look not at fundamental principles of the role of bureaucracy but to refocus effort on driving the existing system towards greater efficiency and stronger political direction. The concept is connected to the generally promulgated view that bureaucracy can have no separate purpose or constitutional position of its own but is simply a tool of the other divisions of power in the state – there to do the bidding of the government of the day within the rules of law established by the legislature and as sustained and tested by the judiciary.

Weber's focus on law and professionalism, however, links to an alternative viewpoint of the nature of bureaucracy as a distinct part of the governance system, the guardian of expertise and rules that sustains the coherence of the modern democratic state, inextricably linked by Weber with achieving mass, rather than localized, forms of democracy. It is this latter viewpoint we turn to in considering the ideas of Woodrow Wilson and the development of the administrative state.

Efficiency or democratic values

Woodrow Wilson

By the time Weber's final work was published, government was already facing the mounting social and environmental implications of the industrializing age. This was prompting consideration of the need for a more flexible, active bureaucracy to meet the pressures of the change from the agrarian economy, rapid urbanization and a changing social order. The idea of a potential active civil society role for bureaucracy was promoted by Lorenz von Stein, Hegel's pupil and Woodrow Wilson's tutor. Von Stein saw the state as a social enterprise not simply an economic one (von Stein, 1958) with public administration as the 'working state', a living organism instead of simply the agent of government (Seibel, 2010). Von Stein published widely on public bureaucracy and advised nation states on governance reforms. As the 28th US president, Woodrow Wilson built on these narratives to set out ideas of a flexible public bureaucracy which has its own role in binding and developing the nation in a civic sense and as a counterweight to economic forces. During his terms in office, Wilson established the Federal Reserve, anti-trust laws and consumer protections.

Woodrow Wilson viewed bureaucracy as a creative civic force which could expressly use its power as a force for minimizing domination. His primary goal was to enable the state to become 'the master of masterful corporations', in a (probably unintentional) nod to the quote from Marx which opens this chapter. His express analogy, however, was still one drawn from the mechanical world of industrial production – of fixing the belts and pulleys as well as the boiler of administration. In his academic article, 'The Study of Administration' (Wilson, 1887), published only a few years after the Pendleton Act had restricted the US spoils system of appointments, Wilson set out the opportunity to have a professional public administration that worked in the public interest. While the text talks of efficiency, Wilson saw the shape and purpose of bureaucracy in America as needing to be intimately connected with supporting its pluralist democratic spirit and constitution: 'The ideal for us is a civil service cultured and self-sufficient enough to act with sense and vigor, and yet so intimately connected with the popular thought, by means of elections and constant public counsel, as to find arbitrariness or class spirit quite out of the question' (Wilson, 1887, 217). And: 'Our duty is, to supply the best possible life to a federal organization, to systems within systems; to make county, city, state and federal governments live with a like strength and an equally assured healthfulness, keeping each unquestionably its own master and yet making all interdependent and co-operative' (Wilson, 1887, 221). Wilson's goals of service to the public, not just superiors, and of avoiding the centralizing uniformity which Weber saw as inherent in mass democracy, place these ideas firmly within a context of how the function and organization of bureaucracy itself can support more inclusive civic governance (Cook, 2007).

Waldo: beyond the administrative state

The orthodox assumptions about bureaucracy as a neutral, technical–scientific pursuit based in efficiency were roundly critiqued by Dwight Waldo in *The Administrative State* (Waldo, 1948). His classic text demonstrates how rather than being a neutral science, the approach to public administration is a political theory and one which, through its focus on efficiency and scientific management as guiding principles, shapes outcomes and structures towards centralization and control rather than democratization. He critiqued the notion of the strict separation of politics and administration, seeing them instead operating with a seamless discretion which needed to be recognized in the context of the operation of the democratic state.

Waldo was a founding father of the concept dubbed New Public Administration which emerged in the late 1960s. In response to what Waldo felt was so absent in the orthodox accounts, New Public Administration offered an ethical democratic purpose for bureaucracy of promoting social equity and democracy through proactivity and advocacy, engaged with civil society and innovative, rather than pursuing a passive neutrality. These views held considerable academic sway over the contested period of the 1970s but have come to be eclipsed in public policy by neoliberal views of the minimalist role of bureaucracy, seeing people not as citizens but customers, and the reassertion of narrow economic efficiency tests as the basis of rational decision-making. New Public Administration's sense of a socially active bureaucracy supported by democratization and decentralization of its role is not so dissimilar from Wilson's and offers a countervailing narrative to the traditional Weberian and Liberal view. It has been picked up in writing on the importance of administrative discretion (such as work on street-level bureaucracy) and in advocacy for a distinct role for public service values in the fabric of governance beyond a mere instrument of either government or the consumer (Denhardt and Denhardt, 2007; Heath, 2020).

Thinking on the distinctive contributions of bureaucracy to the state has not led to establishing a formal constitutional role for bureaucracy as part of the modern form of the executive. This would at first glance be a ready extension of Montesquieu's separation of powers under civic republican thinking, but the primacy of the democratically elected government and legislature identified by Weber is a narrative firmly established as the main source of bureaucratic legitimacy. This was perhaps most starkly stated in the Armstrong memorandum, issued in 1985 by the then Head of the UK Civil Service under the Thatcher government, at a time when bureaucracy was seen as a check on reformist zeal:

> The Civil Service as such has no constitutional personality or responsibility separate from the duly constituted Government of the day. It is there to provide the Government of the day with advice on the formulation of the policies of the Government, to assist in carrying out the decisions of the Government, and to manage and deliver the services for which the Government is responsible. (Armstrong, 1985)

Von Mises' Bureaucracy

The mid-20th-century growth in public bureaucracy was attacked in Von Mises' classic diatribe *Bureaucracy* (Von Mises, 1944) as 'big government' and 'socialism', which is inevitably 'inefficient' and 'self-serving', In this narrative, bureaucracy is seen not as a necessary function of the modern democratic state as in Weber, or as a potentially creative, civic force, but as what is wrong with the modern state. Recalling Weber's concern that a planned economy would need an even bigger bureaucracy and be less efficient, Von Mises offers a classical liberal critique based on bureaucracy becoming a limitation on individual and market freedoms. It represents a call for freedom from government interference against the idea that bureaucracy is central to sustaining mass democracy. William A. Niskanen applied public choice theory to add to the arguments against bureaucracy by positing that both politicians and administrators always act in self-interest and seek to maximize their budgets (Niskanen, 1971). Such critique has underpinned arguments both for small government, and for a focus on the efficiency of government. This narrative has been influential in framing late 20th-century approaches to bureaucratic reform.

Controlling the bureaucracy: the strange rise of managerialism

Waldo criticized the impact of 'scientific management' on public administration, feeling that its theories had virtually become merged. This was a dig at the term coined and popularized in industry at the beginning of the century by F.W. Taylor (Taylor, 1998). Almost coinciding with Waldo's publication, Herbert A. Simon, an advocate of better scientific management in administration and a founder of organization theory, published his book *Administrative Behaviour* (Simon, 1947). The two squared off in an invective filled exchange in the *American Political Science Review* of 1952 largely around the issue of whether it is possible or useful to distinguish the scope of the political executive from the administrative and seek to limit judgements of values ('ought') to one and of fact ('is') to the other (Harmon, 1989). Simon's approach ran directly counter to Waldo's interest in recognizing the potential need for overt democratic values within public administration rather than seeking to reinstate the Weberian separation.

The adoption of practices of management, leadership, human resource and organization theory came to overlay and generally reinforce the control aspects of bureaucracy. Drawn from operational studies in industry, this work takes businesses practices and applies them in a technocratic search for efficiency in the operation and management of public service. Here too, though, there is an intellectual split between controlling and enabling frameworks. Victor A. Thompson, for example, in *Modern Organisation* (Thompson, 1961), identified problems in hierarchical managerial control and focused on the impacts of inappropriate bureaucracy on decision-making and employee behaviour in an increasingly specialized and complex working environment. Human resource and organization theory brought a social eye to scientific management by considering the human not so much as a cog in the machine motivated by personal interest but as a more social animal. Elton Mayo pioneered industrial and organizational psychology that formed the basis for concepts in human resources. In his unironically titled 1933 book *The Human Problems of an Industrialised Civilisation* (Mayo, 1977), he focused on how to make groups of workers more efficient, considering working practices and incentives. This work influenced thinking on the need for management of people not just of work and for a broader understanding of the social dimension of work. In bureaucracy this fed into the adoption of formalized incentive, progression and accountability structures, designed to motivate desired behaviours and approaches to the delivery of work, but still based in reinforcing the neutral rather than democratic view of the role of public administration.

Managerialism remains highly influential in forms of governance practice and its focus on efficiency can still come to replace other governance values and becomes a narrative end in itself. As Waldo argued, it begs the question as to the purpose of this efficiency and whether one efficiency is hermetically sealed from other efficiencies. I think inevitably in this context of the UK New Labour mantra of 'doing what works' and the associated 'What works' network set up with UK government support in academia.

Recent bureaucratic reform narratives

In the late 20th century, as part of the wider neoliberal turn of government, New Public Management combined neoliberal marketization with managerialist ideas to address the perceived inefficiency of bureaucracy and the challenge of keeping up with growing public demands upon the welfare state (Hood, 1991). These ideas remain a prominent framing of bureaucratic reform in many countries and for international bodies and form an underlaying fabric even where more networked governance has been embraced using ideas of New Public Governance (Osborn, 2010). Indeed, New Public Governance can be seen not so much as its own reform agenda but as an attempt to address the breakdown of bureaucratic governance caused by New Public Management.

The focus of New Public Management is on privatization of functions to introduce market discipline, coupled with matrices of performance management to deliver efficiency in what remains within the public sector. All of this is set within the narrative of the supposed (fiscal) unaffordability and (social and economic) inefficiency of the welfare state. These attempts at reform can be characterized as seeking both to address the principal–agent question in which bureaucracy is seen as a barrier to the implementation of political will and to slim down the public sector through market efficiencies. It offered:

- focus on targetry, incentivizing the existing system better to deliver specific outputs;
- competitive funding mechanisms such as specific grants or internal cost centres;
- application of specific fashionable approaches such as Total Quality Management, Balanced Scorecard, project management, outsourcing, marketing, human resources etc as 'the answer';
- predominance of economic techniques and business prioritization in decision-making;
- a sense that complexity can be addressed through a combination of the use of markets and outcome frameworks.

These recent reformist critiques are still set within the frame of political economy but, in contrast to the mid-20th-century arguments, see a more limited role for government in the social and civic sphere, presenting bureaucracy as having a limited delivery role, easily substituted by the market. Here the broad concept of the officer's service to the public – as called upon by Woodrow Wilson – mutates to become the efficient delivery of prescribed public services to individuals. Such shifting of language matters, but it is too easy for careless use of narratives to capture the weary and unwary bureaucrat or politician.

New Public Management has reinforced a narrow business efficiency argument over wider discussion and reflection on the role and operation of public administration (Savoie, 1994). Meanwhile, alternative voices such as Denhardt and Denhardt have influenced but perhaps not shifted the ground of public service delivery and bureaucratic practice (Denhardt and Denhardt, 2015). In the early years of this century, the impact of narratives of New Public Management, right populism and austerity has left bureaucracy to be presented chiefly as a barrier to partisan government within the frame of competitive democracy, self-interested and inefficient, and accused of 'not working for the people', rather than as the potential champion – or at least honest broker – for the wider polity envisaged by Wilson and Waldo.

The bureaucratic experience

From my experience, and in my interviews with leading figures in the Welsh legislative experience (see Appendix 5) about the barriers to governing for sustainable development, the dominant character of the practice of bureaucracy is still markedly Weberian, overlaid by the pressures of managerialist tools and the reduction in direct capacity undertaken in the name of austerity. Considering the self-reproductive nature of governmentality, a bureaucracy which is itself unreflexive, siloed, rule-bound, short-term and subject to managerial and market pressures seems unlikely to be able to foster a civil society and governance system which is anything but a mirror of itself. It is reproducing an order which is a poor fit with our understanding of the world as complex interactive systems. This suggests the purpose of bureaucracy needs not to be simply the guardian of the economic efficiency of the state but that its role needs to be set within a broader rationality that embraces the social and environmental functioning of society and the health of the wider polity. This is presently constrained, in Foucault's terms, by the practice of governmentality guided by political economy.

Knowledge-power

In both Weber and Foucault, the legitimation of bureaucracy is drawn from its exercise of technical, professional knowledge in its formal decision-making processes and in its exercise of professional judgement.

The two main expressions of knowledge-power within bureaucracy are professional disciplines and the practice of metric power, largely through forms of economic and statistical analysis.

Economic tests are generally a required part of major spending programmes, schemes and projects. The most notable example is the use of forms of cost–benefit analysis. This encapsulates the economic efficiency goal of the state by seeking to establish numerically that benefits to society in general outweigh government costs of implementation. It is often accompanied by option appraisal where one aim is to test whether a government intervention is merited at all due to some form of market failure. The results of numerical analysis are generally subject to discounting based on time preference theory. The way in which cost–benefit analysis is generally applied in bureaucracy sums up the constraining power of such economic tests.

The process of establishing the new single environmental body in Wales – what became Natural Resources Wales – Cyfoeth Naturiol Cymru – provides an example of the impact of business planning tools. The genesis of the change came from internal policy work on the benefits of an ecological rather than conservation and regulatory approach to environment and nature. Action was catalysed by practical issues arising from divergent policy between England and Wales for the direction of the shared agencies – the Environment Agency and the Forestry Commission – and the opportunity to legislate was provided by the UK coalition government's Public Bodies Act – the vehicle for its own cull of quangos.

The move from policy concept to implementation required two business cases – one in the last term of the outgoing Welsh Labour–Plaid Cymru coalition government (2009–11) and a further one after the commitment to create the body had been included in three of the political parties' manifestos and taken up by the new Welsh Labour administration (2011–16). The business case required options appraisal, financial and cost–benefit analyses and the application of programme optimism bias. Through the application of these processes, the emphasis shifted from the original rationale for the establishment of the body (matching the new long-term legal policy framework) to determining how the body could be established and run within existing budgetary constraints and demonstrate a positive financial net present value. The media and politicians were much more able to pick up on the published efficiencies claimed for the new body than discuss the new policy rationale. It was tracking these notional savings that became the driving force of the scrutiny of the body in its early years and which set the initial tone for staff and management. What had started as a means to create a joined-up, reflexive, participatory organization considering all aspects of the sustainable use of land, air and water had turned into an efficiency narrative and created a self-limiting and internally focused narrative for the new body. The internal milieu had fed a corresponding external milieu that constrained the new body in its activities and its style of operation for several years.

Knowledge-power based on professional disciplines remains a strong feature of modern bureaucracy. These are often aligned with departmental structures and the associated legal requirements and technical bases for policy and decision-making. As part of steps to develop staff training in support of the new legislative framework in Wales, my institute organized two pilot trainings in 2019 in place-based co-production for staff of the Welsh Government and Natural Resources Wales. The idea was to introduce officials to wider tools of engagement and to encourage them to shed some of their technical and controlling processes and assumptions and engage in a more empathetic response. The use of place was helpful in allowing participants to relate to their own experiences and to connect issues but the role-playing in the first session brought out controlling approaches to expertise that were a near perfect live example of the exercise of knowledge-power based in the application of professional expertise. Colleagues also struggled to understand how they could use the new ways of working in making cases for action because they did not represent the expected metric power required for business cases. In the second pilot we added a module on 'unlearning' which explained the narrow focus of the present metric power they were exercising and provided a case for the legitimacy of other forms of knowledge and how that could be part of new processes.

Territory

Management of territory is a central element for Foucault of the systemic factors which control the milieu. The British land use planning system was established with the stated goal of managing the use and development of land in the public interest. This system concerns itself only with assigning development land and formed part of a post-war set of acts that also established National Parks and regulation of forestry and agricultural land. While the land use planning profession has argued that sustainable development is at its core, it has found itself prey to different interpretations of what it means to develop sustainably (Owens and Cowell, 2002).

The land use planning system also has economic efficiency at its heart. It seeks to reproduce particular forms of economic activity and social organisation. It places requirements on local planning authorities to provide for high capacity, low-cost urban and semi-urban housing development and the needs of retail, office and business space while minimizing development in smaller rural areas and designating the more remote land as farming and forestry. This reinforces the uniformity of the urban and the structural separation between the urban and nature, rurality and food.

This deterritorialization for economic provision and uniformity sits in tension with wider social and environmental goals. The focus on economic agglomeration and urbanism meant that the local and rural scale was largely disregarded or considered an area of exception.

The Wales Spatial Plan (WG, 2004b) was a statutory spatial planning process intended to set spatial priorities for all Welsh Government activity and to guide land use planning. The plan was set in the context of achieving sustainable development and was a forerunner of later legislative and institutional work. The plan was developed through working groups with central and local officials and agencies in a series of informal regional geographical areas. These reported to ministerially chaired working groups with senior officials and local politicians, alongside wider stakeholder engagement events. The plan's guiding principles were a direct challenge to economic efficiency and uniformity. They were: building sustainable communities; promoting a sustainable economy; valuing our environment; achieving sustainable access; and respecting distinctiveness.

The first plan was supported by regular meetings of representatives in each region chaired by a senior official or minister. The groups were able to set and monitor spatial priorities for strategic direction and investment. I chaired several awkward meetings where departmental officers were exposed by the process to the spatial implications of their centralized decisions, most memorably in North Wales on the very urban South Wales focus of housing policy.

The work foundered not long after its first update in 2008. Subsequent ministers and senior officials had not brought in to the process and had no interest in the plan guiding their sectoral decisions. Central officials also struggled with tailoring approaches to differing spatial priorities. The Welsh Government professional planning department had little engagement with the process and did not own the steering logic of the plan, reverting to a traditional predict and provide, trend-based intervention in planning work.

This culminated in their directing more housing growth into Cardiff when the Spatial Plan had stated that this should largely be diverted into the wider region, linked to planned public transport investment.

While the plan had a statutory basis, this had too major limitations. It was not specifically binding on the Welsh Government itself in its actions; and there was no element in the statute to underpin the participative process and give it weight in decision-making.

The experiment demonstrated that the momentum of decision-making based in sectoral and professional thinking and departmental discretion was strong enough to cut across statutory spatial deliberative processes. The conventional tools of uniformity, predict and provide planning, budgetary discretion of departments and central control militated against place-based governance for sustainability.

The extent of the mismatch of the planning system with governance for sustainable development was further demonstrated in the One Planet Living planning policy of the Welsh Government. This was developed by the Welsh Government planning department, with the aid of planning consultants, in response to the political wish to regularize an unregulated low environmental impact community development in rural West Wales. The eventual policy offered the general prospect of obtaining planning permission for ultra-low impact development. This was caveated by the requirement to meet and sustain a stringent series of conditions and give detailed regular reporting on how the properties were being used in order to demonstrate their minimal environmental impact. The accompanying guidance (WG, 2012b) runs to 71 pages and the conditions are much more stringent than for any other form of development. This is justified on the basis that the policy allows for development which is an exception to general planning policy.

It is striking that for a more sustainable, ecologically based form of development to be accepted into the system, it was necessary to place significant barriers to developing this alternative, environmentally friendly development, and this at the same time as the system continued to place few environmental requirements, beyond site mitigation, on major development.

Institutional structures: departmentalism

The bounded departmentalism of Weberian bureaucracy is alive and well in modern civil service structures and has in part been exacerbated by the number of arm's-length agencies and delivery bodies which tend to face their own sectors or audiences. Departmentalism due to the structures of bureaucracy presents a major barrier to the systemic thinking needed for sustainable development and to the ability to work through decentralized, place-based forms of governance.

The operation of separate, planning, funding and performance systems by each department in Wales effectively reproduced national siloes at the lower tiers of government and across agencies and civil society. This militated against the intended working across local services and the sharing of budgets to address issues with a place-based sensitivity and engagement. My interview discussants in Wales pointed to the resulting combative relationship with local government. Attempts at collaboration across levels of government had proved difficult; 'we're on the ground' versus 'but we know best' and were described in gendered terms as: 'blokes shouting'.

The siloed nature of bureaucracy places a premium on co-ordination mechanisms. When asked to describe what I did as a senior civil servant, my most frequent reply was that I chaired or attended meetings. The New Labour UK government (1997–2010) adopted the aim of 'joined-up government' to move from co-ordination to common purpose (Kavanagh and Richards, 2001) in addressing the siloed, bounded impact of departmentalism. This appealed to me to the extent that a close colleague once quipped that if I were to be sliced like a stick of British seaside candy you would read the running motto 'Joined up Government' rather than 'Greetings from Blackpool'. New Labour attempted a variation on conventional hierarchical targetry to create this common purpose through introducing Public Service Agreements where more than one department might hold responsibility for deliverables, but this had little impact in the closing period of the administration (Panchamia and Thomas, 2014).

The barriers were most acute when trying to pull together a policy statement that cut across large numbers of departments. One experienced senior colleague in Wales joked that assembling different contributions felt like passing the hat round, though with the likelihood that you wouldn't get the hat back! In other words, you may have contributions but the guiding rationale for action would be lost. Another senior civil servant regularly commented in relation to the aspirations for sustainable development that "you can't join up everything", as if separation of issues were a natural state.

Where a common, or at least coherent, approach was felt to be needed, the tendency was to reach for compliance checklists. My Strategic Policy Unit team in Wales attempted to build on this approach by creating a formal appraisal process to encourage departments to consider the implications of their proposals for other areas of policy. Produced with the support of the NGO, Forum for the Future, the tool was used as the basis for a cross-office seminar which was held on each major policy initiative to identify, and hopefully improve, the fit with other governmental goals. The results of the seminar were then presented as a spider diagram in any public consultations on the proposal.

The approach eventually fell into disuse after I left strategic policy. It often came too late to influence the process of decision-making, could be avoided by departments, and its published results – intended as an opportunity for transparency and accountability – did not stimulate any public or parliamentary questions. The extent of formal compliance processes across the Welsh Government and pressure on time meant attempts at processes to encourage coherence of policy development generally led to tick-box responses.

Narratives

Public service delivery and performance

When I began my bureaucratic career, the focus of performance was very much on testing the long-term effectiveness of policy direction. There were still one-off and standing Royal Commissions to take an independent view of effectiveness. I was fortunate to work closely with the Royal Commission on Environmental Pollution (RCEP) in its work on reviewing policy effectiveness or pointing to new issues that needed to be addressed. This included the coruscating Transport and Environment Report of 1994 which spelled out the incompatibility of transport policy with environmental aspirations. Such long-term advisory bodies have been axed from the UK scene in preference for short-term performance management against government-set targets. The RCEP was closed in 2011 under the UK coalition government's cull of public bodies. The Audit Commission (which supported local authority improvement) and the Sustainable Development Commission were also among long-standing and influential advisory and review bodies to fall in the same cull.

In the place of this focus on broad effectiveness of governance has come a focus on the minutiae of short-term delivery based in efficiency. This combination of managerialism and a focus on centralized driving in a principal-agent model of bureaucratic governance has been reflected in thinking on public accountability and in particular the managerialist approach which seeks to tie down every aspect of bureaucratic delivery through very specific targets and incentives. This narrowly defined accountability restricts the ability to adjust spending, service or regulatory activities once they are set and can create perverse incentives and results (Pollitt, 2000).

The guiding narrative of public service delivery, drawn from New Public Management, was a powerful controlling idea within Welsh Government bureaucracy. Discussant officials saw it as part of a drive towards uniformity and performance control: "We always think we know what's best because we can't tolerate local variation." Ministers concurred that a "postcode lottery [in services] is not acceptable". Central direction had an appeal even to those who saw the pitfalls: "The Stalinist in me likes targets" and "We need to be China for a day." Yet practitioners knew that managerialism was an unhelpful focus in a complex environment: "targets and KPIs can drive dysfunctional behaviour". Civil society colleagues viewed the delivery mantra as a barrier and challenged the centralizing economic efficiency argument: "The public service delivery mantra is really problematic – it is top down and closes doors. Is that the only purpose of government?"

The systems of control were also inimical to the forms of bottom-up participative governance seen by practitioners as necessary to governing for sustainable development. The administrator was focused on applying existing process, structures and safeguards rather than enabling outcomes and adaptative management. Officials were defensive of their own areas of control and defended individual grants over unhypothecated funding for local government or enabling funding for civil society. There was an increasing reluctance by central government to fund the intermediary bodies and supporting processes that could build capacity and relationship across civil society. The efficiency focus pulled against the arguments for governing for civic participation and as funds grew tighter and the delivery narrative stronger, supporting processes of civil society were viewed as not contributing to delivery. This was reflected in grants being increasingly focused on specific deliverables, resulting in a cut-throat NGO sector focused heavily on survival. The degree of direction from central government, coupled with funding requirements, generated a 'learned helplessness' in some and an 'elastic clientelism' in others that undermined the potential democratizing, pluralistic force of civic participation.

Accountability and risk

As well as shaping the internal milieu, the focus on delivery failure and narrow accountability that was the stuff of competitive democracy impacted on civil society, as one former minister put it: "the blame game erodes public belief". This pressure could be exacerbated by civil society engagement. With some notable exceptions, external engagement from NGOs was seen as focused "mainly on sticks" – creating specific accountabilities and holding government to account for failure rather than building strategic dialogue. Parliamentarians and the media reinforced this accountability narrative. The extent of requirements for reporting got in the way of delivery or, as one mid-ranking official put it in conversation: "You can't do it because you keep having to say you are doing it."

The atmosphere created by senior management and politicians shaped the degree of risk aversion, and a collaborative or control focus. Former ministers praised the style of government fostered by the late First Minister Rhodri Morgan who loved ideas, was interested in different views, and never defensive or controlling. This was seen in contrast to senior officials in the early days of devolution who adopted a risk-averse stance, defining success as 'not dropping the ball', prioritizing avoiding the impact of a failure in the new organization over innovation.

Neutrality and objectivity

Despite the supposed and often voiced neutrality and technocracy of bureaucracy, both ministers and officials acknowledged that individual departments had their own cultures, sometimes rooted in different disciplines. Staff could build careers in those same structures and associate themselves with those cultures and values. Although the technocratic structures and tools created an in-built focus on political economy and competition, the lack of express values left considerable scope for independent framing by bureaucrats. This might often be expressed as 'skirt-hiding' by officials under the guise of 'the minister won't like that'. Officials were identified as having their own individual views, with some senior officials seen as having a 'visceral opposition' to sustainable development in the conversations with civil society figures.

All practitioners in discussion viewed officials as risk-averse and incremental, lacking creative or imaginative capacity. One official talked about administrators having had the "magical thinking" drummed out of them by a system which valued analytical thinking, abstraction and numerical measurement, while ministers were attracted to "eye catching initiatives which sound excellent". This combination left politicians frustrated by lack of creativity and officials frustrated by a lack of thinking through of proposals. Another official linked the lack of bureaucratic creativity to control and bounded rationality, stressing the lack of self-reflexion or self-awareness in public administration, coupled with the human mind seeking self-confirmation not contrary evidence. This meant there was, as one official put it: "a huge untapped potential not being put to work".

Public administrators are also often a poor reflexion of the diversity of experience. Senior offices are populated by people who attended elite universities (I put my hand up) or expensive schools. Public administration struggles to enable the use of diverse skills and approaches within its rule- and norm-based approach. I remember vividly the induction meetings for staff who had been merged into the newly established Welsh Executive. The Public Health meeting was particularly horrific when a senior member of staff told them upfront that they had been big fish in a small pond and were now a cog in the larger machine. Neither the traditional focus on policy design nor the recent push for business and project delivery skills has put much emphasis on 'non-technical' skills such as reflection or empathy.

The combination of departmental cultures, incrementality and individual sense-making by officials weakened the extent to which departments bought in to collective decisions or embraced new priorities or behaviours. This was one of the reasons why Welsh ministers ultimately decided on creating a stronger legal base for sustainable development as the express values for judging action.

Government of the day

The mantra of the UK civil service code is that officials serve the public by serving the government of the day. Under present norms, public administrators have no clear or express democratic or civil role. Those roles are enshrined in representative democracy. Processes of executive governmental engagement of all forms with civil society are mainly conducted through public administration with bureaucrats seen simply as ministerial agents. Public bureaucracy is generally held to be the servant of the (democratically elected or otherwise) political masters of the day. While some roles have specific, if limited, legal protections from political control or influence, public servants are only servants of the public by proxy under this system.

Sensitivity to the ministerial vibe is a learnt skill of public servants and can create a pressure to tell ministers what they want to hear and at least is self-limiting on what advice is put forward. It also gives ministers who wish to exercise their power significant scope to impact on the careers of public servants. The sayings 'the face doesn't fit' or 'I don't want that person in a meeting again' were at times prevalent during my career and saw staff moved on or to other areas of work.

One senior colleague put it that ministers seemed only to like rebels or plodders – mavericks who could get things done for them despite the system or traditional officials who turned the handle on the machine. One former minister cast the appropriate relationship between bureaucrats and politicians in the classic principal–agent model of ministers having big ideas and officials managing the detailed steps.

Discussants identified an unresolved tension in the public servant role of serving the government of the day with the desired bottom-up participation in decision-making. Representative politics always trumped participative democracy. This occurred at local authority as well as central government level and led to tensions with civil society, captured in discussion by the phrase: "Who do these people think they are? I've been elected."

Current expressions of representative democracy were seen by some discussants as a barrier to the application in full of the concept of achieving genuine co-production between civil society and public administration. Officials agreed that in order for anything to make sense "you must give people say in design of things that affect them", or, as one civil society leader put it more strongly: "I have an inherent belief that bottom-up visions of self-shaping local futures and families is at the heart of [governing for sustainable development]. Ownership gives well-being as opposed to being 'done to'." Bureaucrats, however, had concern about the lack of clear legitimacy in public administration occupying this intermediary space below the elected politicians and also feared the evident risk of technocratic capture of the process of engagement by the bureaucrats, a lived experience of civil society discussants. As one official concluded, however: "It needs something in the space between the ballot box every four years."

The primacy of representative politics in the current framing of bureaucracy undermines the aim that the exercise of power should be part of a wider civic dialogue or that power be more widely shared through deliberative mechanisms or local determination. This reinforces a process of domination and centralized decision-making.

Discipline

The checks on bureaucratic activity served to act as a discipline on the ability to move from efficiency and control to more reflexive and enabling forms. The main disciplinary tests applied in bureaucracy reinforce the narrow economic and bounded sectoral thinking. In my discussions with colleagues, it was the framework of financial controls, based on the duties of value for money and propriety, that were clearest for disciplining the way the bureaucrat could work. Monies are delegated for specific areas of work and delegations of authority given to spend that money. Some financial decisions, such as the award of large grants, require ministerial approval, others are fully delegated but subject to separation of approvals to avoid the risk of fraud. Central finance teams hold considerable sway. They advise the finance minister on how the funding should be allocated between departments. They determine and oversee processes of business case approval and they set the, very largely economic, tools that are used to make financial decisions. Finance departments and Treasuries are probably the most influential in determining the limits of possibility through the metrics and tools they apply to decision-making. Central financial controls generate a raft of rules and reporting, accounting and audit requirements which discipline both the internal and the external milieu, for example through rules and general practice on grants awards and management.

External audit is a major tool of control on the nature of decision-making and tends to support a narrow focus on efficiency and propriety. It is nearly irreconcilable with reflexivity and uncertainty in what and how it currently tests. In 2012, the UK government culled the Audit Commission, whose role was improvement, while retaining the National Audit Office, whose role is oversight of propriety and value for money. Wales opted instead to merge its commission into the more adversarial audit office role. While the new body continued to produce broad improvement reports, it is the short studies and specific interventions which discipline behaviour as they have a formal process for departmental sign-off and can be examined by the Parliament. Audit acts as the enforcer for process rules of procurement and grant.

Imaginative attempts to develop community leasehold ownership of the local landscape of former coal mining areas in the South Wales Valleys (Project Skyline) was stymied in 2020 when the Auditor General raised issues regarding generalized procurement restrictions on the actions of the public agency involved. What started as an idea of giving local control over the social, environmental and economic benefits of these landscapes, including generating income for the deprived communities, became filleted to giving them a small grant, no opportunity for income and just a say over how the public agency undertook its management.

The allocation of budgets to departments and to their specific responsibilities reinforced departmentalism and meant that collaboration across portfolios was considered challenging, or as a senior official stated:"budgets drive a narrowness through individuals." Existing mechanisms of co-ordination across departments did not work to focus attention on underlying challenges due to the strong functional and internal competitive nature of the structures. Discussants felt that this would require task or place-based working on root causes that would reveal their complexity and interlinkage.

The award from 2018 of significant additional borrowing approvals to address coastal flooding risk in Wales provided an opportunity to explore the scope for traditionally technical engineering infrastructure to generate multiple benefits. Building on the success of a fortuitous overlap with regeneration funding which had enabled a comprehensive approach to renewal on part of the North Wales coast, the programme was devised as a multi-objective offer to local authorities. A formal programme board involving colleagues from other departments, agencies and local government was established to oversee its development. The department visited regional meetings of local authority chief executives to encourage them to promote the potential of the broader scope.

Several issues arose in the programme's development. Most first stage scheme proposals were led by flood engineers and demonstration of wider benefits was limited. Those schemes which had an economic development lead in contrast failed to demonstrate sufficient flood benefit. The internal financial authority to spend money on activities outside the remit of the department was unclear – the programme had to develop its own rule of thumb approach of a *de minimis* sliding scale before funding had to come from other departments or sources.

The attempt demonstrated that the financial and delivery structures were not only not designed to deliver multiple benefits but severely hindered multiple outcomes. This meant that the degree of co-ordination and promotional effort needed to establish funding programmes of this sort was disproportionately high compared to a conventional single purpose approach. This in turn increased the lead time, making the scheme a poor fit with the financial and political cycles.

The lure of the controlling practice of grant awards was revealed in attempts in my department to shift to more creative forms of funding to match the reflexivity needed for the new well-being and ecological frameworks under development. The Nature Fund was a sum of grant funding quickly assembled for the then Environment Minister for launch in 2014 as a response to the RSPB's State of Nature report (RSPB, 2013). As the idea coincided with participative strategy development with nature stakeholders (set in the context of the proposals for the Well-being Act), the opportunity was taken to create an open two-stage process with an initial call for ideas in which the only conditions were that the proposal would be developed in partnership over a local area and would address multiple aspects of ecological resilience with potential for wider societal benefits. Paperwork was minimal and each proposal should determine its own performance criteria rather than there being a prescribed list. In the second stage, officials would work with proposals to ensure they were legally compliant.

The original proposal had no prior spatial priorities but in response to a political aspiration for action areas (mimicking English proposals), the first stage proposals were used as the basis for announcing geographically broad action areas for stage 2. Funding was extremely time limited. Established NGOs chafed at the requirements for fostering local partnership, captured in one NGO figure commenting to me: "you give me the money, and I'll find the partners". The department organized locally based information and training sessions to help build partnerships and the understanding of partnership working. The department then held regular network sessions with the successful participants and commissioned a specific appraisal process to capture the wider and emergent benefits and issues of the programme.

Over the period of the grant, two further ministers had responsibility. They held different views and priorities to the originating minister and decisions on awards to specific proposals were delayed. The final minister closed the scheme early. The fund was succeeded by funding supported through EU programmes which shifted the balance to a more audit-based approach. This was subsequently replaced under the next minister by focused grants on specific topic areas.

The experience showed that the competitive (for efficiency) and directive (for uniformity) norms of grant bidding as 'beauty contest' for specific deliverables is very embedded. The participative and reflexive process adopted for the grants was uncomfortable for both ministers and traditional bidders and there was a subsequent reversion to traditional formats. Existing approaches to evaluation were unable to be used to appraise the programme as they presumed a fixed and consistent set of performance measures rather than allowing reflexivity or emergence.

Taking stock

There are fundamental issues in the inherited model of control in the face of the transformatory call of sustainable development and the challenges of a post-truth populism. Underlying its lack of fitness for the modern era are:

- an inability to reflect whole system issues when each operational unit is essentially separated and in competition;
- focus on economic, financial and statistical tools and measures;
- a desire for certainty and planned outcomes;
- a desire to control and to rationalize complexity;
- focus on technical expertise over general or local experience and knowledge;
- one-size-fits-all standardized approaches that do not allow for differentiation for place or circumstance or allow connections with others;
- a reluctance to share power, limiting the ability to work openly with others internally or externally to increase understanding and engagement;
- status-based professional condescension for views of ordinary people or subordinates.

Bureaucratic norms and structures based on rational technocratic control (knowledge-power) and order (discipline) are now expressed in the uniformity of managerialism (which denies self-organization) and of neoliberal contracting out (which prescribes the metrics of delivery). These still serve to reinforce control and siloed organization at the expense of the ability to make wider connections, collaborate and address broader societal outcomes (Denhardt and Denhardt, 2015). These same limitations are expressed in the frustration and mistrust of government, science and democracy. The centralizing and controlling behaviour of bureaucrats disempower citizens and disconnects them from civic life. The managerialist lack of trust in the ability of others to act without direction breeds corresponding distrust within and of governance. The lack of respect for other forms of knowledge, such as local understandings, is patronizing and closes the possibility of understanding richer views and wider connections. The reliance on process over communication keeps bureaucrats and, in turn, government distant, impenetrable and impersonal. The main bureaucratic roles which confront the majority of citizens remain those ancient ones of the impersonal tax collector, accountant and issuer of licences.

Almost all the approval systems of governmental and business action are regulated by processes drawn from the economic or financial world. Increasingly, bureaucratic systems have become fuelled by and dependent upon predictive models, statistical method and scenarios that can provide some pretence of a structured basis for decision-making within a complex world. These practices exercise a 'metric power' (Beer, 2016) and determine the rules of the game (Desrosières, 2002), be it public enquiries into road schemes or commercial investment decisions. In seeking to standardize and regularize, they tend to dehumanize decision-making and close off argument. This is a far cry from Wilson, Waldo or Foucault and Pettit's calls.

Bureaucracy: a civic ecosystem in place of mechanical efficiency?

Just as Woodrow Wilson envisaged a new role for public administration in forging America in the early 20th century (Wilson, 1887), so sustainable development and the related challenges of the 21st century calls for a rethinking of our narratives of what is normal and right if bureaucracy is to be fit for new purpose and re-legitimized in its exercise of power in the public interest.

When I interviewed former colleagues who in different roles (ministers, officials, civil society figures) had been intimately involved with the Welsh experience of sustainable development, I invited each in my second question to set out what they felt was important to governing for sustainable development, without defining the term. I received two main answers, one focused on the form of governance and the other on means to achieve it. The first stressed the need for reflexive and localized participative governance as a basis for co-creative, place-based, joined-up and long-term decision-taking. The second focused on the need for strong direction within the public sector to establish new narratives and practices in order to re-orientate governance to the delivery of sustainable development.

All were clear that existing governance narratives and bureaucratic practice would not create the basis for governance for sustainable development. They differed primarily in relation to the emphasis on the importance of participative governance or on change in the mechanics of governing. The first group trusted that locally driven, participative governance was key to addressing sustainable development successfully, while the latter group shared a sense that the power of central authority would need to be applied differently to create and maintain this new framework and to establish new practice.

Colleagues used language which described forms of deliberative and enabling governance. This included recognizing a strong spatial component in which governance was bottom-up, locally determined and place-based. They also emphasized the elements needed instead of existing practice: the need for practice which was joined-up, integrated, reflexive and outcome-focused. Lastly, they employed the language of civic dialogue, stressing involvement, engagement and co-production.

Those who focused more on controlling the governance framework and bureaucratic practices to enable non-domination talked of the need for new processes, practices and ways of measuring. They sought consistent leadership and new narratives, emphasizing social justice and environmental limits, and called for strong frameworks for civic participation.

It is civic republicanism that can offer a guide for considering an enabling role and design of bureaucracy while ensuring it does not become a competing political undertaking. The civic republican concern for designing governance for *sustaining* the republic sets it apart from viewpoints which take a strong specific ethical value as to the purpose of governance *within* a republic. Civic republicanism, based in the egalitarian and communitarian nature of republican citizenship, invites a plurality of views. Various political and ethical considerations are intended to flow from the civic engagement and checks and balances of civic republicanism, but they are the varying and dynamic products, not the purpose, of civic republican organization. Considered in this way, Berlin's classic critique of positive liberty (non-domination) as a route to potential bureaucratic oppression (Berlin, 1969) can, I believe, be negated.

As we consider the nature of governing for sustainable development and take the analogy of an ecological not of an industrial process, there is the possibility of changing the focus of bureaucracy to one of underpinning the conditions for civic change and enabling the reflexive self-governance of complexity, instead of bureaucracy remaining in the mire of attempting to need to be seen to 'solve' complexity by reducing it to meaningless simplifications and easy answers for the government of the day.

The next chapter sets out practical experience of reshaping bureaucracy to this new civic purpose drawn from attempts at applying the concept of governing *for* sustainable development in law.

4

Lessons from governing
for sustainable development

> Deliberate destabilization of established ways of doing things – even in the absence of the possibility of imposing a new equilibrium – can be a crucial resource of reformers.
>
> James Meadowcroft

We have seen how existing bureaucratic frames are deeply rooted in the goal of economic efficiency and the desire for control, order and planned uniformity. They are constrained by a structure, toolkit and narratives designed for and on the model of industrial capitalism which seek to remove complexity and ignore or downplay dynamic linkages between society, economy and environment. This has contributed to a milieu in which individual consumption and power are the purpose of life and economic growth the mantra of governance. They have bred a competitive democracy that seems unable to adapt and is now at risk from the siren call of totalitarianism, fed by disconnect from civic life and a nostalgia for old certainties. The mechanistic growth and efficiency model is incompatible with the reflexivity, uncertainty and localized discussion and decisions which are needed to govern for the systemic challenges of sustainable development.

If bureaucracy is to play a part in change, it needs to reflect a primary civic republican aim of building a strong and pluralistic civil society in which everyone, and, in this modern era, also the social and natural world in which we live, are reconnected, rather than enabling systemic dominations. This means bureaucracy itself needs to abandon the industrial analogue of technocratic control and measures of efficiency, siloed division into topics and bounded rationality to be able to mirror instead the ecological analogy of dynamic interconnected socio-ecological systems. This will enable new narratives and considerations to have voice and power within a participative, place-based and reflexive approach. To do this bureaucracy will need to be equipped with express purpose, new narratives, institutions, ways of knowing and measuring and tools. We can identify emergent forms of these alternatives in experiments in governing for sustainable development.

Governing for sustainable development: the Well-being of Future Generations (Wales) Act 2015

Contextualizing the Welsh case

Wales is a largely rural, upland, coastal and post-industrial nation of three million people and is one of the constituent countries of the United Kingdom. The 1999 National Assembly for Wales (since 2020 renamed as the Senedd or Welsh Parliament) was the first parliament in Wales for almost 600 years. The independent legal system of Wales had been abolished by Henry VIII and laws were subsequently made in the Westminster Parliament for England and Wales. From the 1960s until 1999 Wales had been run from London with a Secretary of State for Wales appointed in the UK Cabinet and a Welsh Office based in London and in the Welsh capitol, Cardiff. The bulk of operational administration was undertaken by a series of large agencies, notably the Welsh Development Agency, leading the governance of Wales to be dubbed a 'quangocracy' and devolution to the Welsh Assembly seen as an exercise in democratizing the quango state. There was therefore more civic focus on the nature of the new democratic settlement (Osmond, 1998) than in the very different contexts of Scotland (which had retained its own legal and judicial structures from the 1706–7 Acts of Union) and Northern Ireland (where the Assembly was established as a central part of the Peace Process).

As a constituent part of the United Kingdom, Wales is not a UN member state, but, as James Meadowcroft reminds us: 'federalism allows experimentation and provides a context where sub-national units can act to address issues that are not yet "mature" on the national scene' (Meadowcroft, 2007, 307). This recalls the civic republican perspective that a diverse multi-level governance in which there is a degree of freedom of action allows for different ideas to flourish.

Frustrations

Despite the efforts of my Welsh Government policy team, the Welsh Government's general legal duty to produce a scheme after each election showing how it would pursue sustainable development in the carrying out of its functions remained stubbornly a legal duty among many. Each formal review of the statutory schemes made under the legal provision showed how far we were coming up short and how little an impact it was making across government. As the examples in the previous chapter have shown, each step forward seemed to be followed by a lurch backwards. For all the interesting work we had pursued both domestically and internationally, I finally came to feel that I had exhausted what I could bring to the strategic policy role. As a co-ordinating division, we seemed to have responsibility for everything and authority over nothing.

In 2006, towards the end of the second Welsh Assembly, I took the option of moving to head the environment team, safe in the knowledge that I would have authority to act over those topics within the remit. In little more than a year, though, sustainable development itself was back among my responsibilities. I found myself heading a new Directorate for Environment, Sustainability and Housing under the former Education Minister, Jane Davidson, who was interested in international thinking and eager to make an impact in the new departmental brief in what turned out to be her last spell as an Assembly member (Davidson, 2020). One product of this term was the final formal scheme under the old legislation – *One Wales: One Planet* (WG, 2009) – which adopted the goal of living within the planet's means and set out that sustainable development was the central organizing principle for Welsh Government. Following a series of flagship achievements on recycling performance, the introduction of a single-use bag charge and the development of an all-Wales coastal path, the last significant policy product of the term was a programme of change in thinking on the environment, termed *A Living Wales*. This took promoting ecological resilience as the main aim of environment policy and of future institutional organization. The central organizing principle would lead to what became the Well-being of Future Generations (Wales) Act 2015 (the Well-being Act) and *A Living Wales* resulted in the accompanying Environment (Wales) Act 2016 and the establishment of a new agency, Natural Resources Wales.

The Well-being Act constitutes the only comprehensive attempt internationally – at least of which I am aware – to reflect in law the notion of governing *for* Sustainable Development, specifically reshaping the goals and values of bureaucratic governance. The explicit aim was to use legislation to tackle the frustration of progress by the existing form and practice of decision-making and the values and practices which lay behind them.

Development of the Act

The Act owes its existence to a special set of circumstances. Not only was the Welsh Government still a new institution with a new legal basis and aspirations to democratization but it was also acquiring additional powers and responsibilities it wished to exercise. The proposal for legislation, alongside action on environment policy and institutions, was included in the Welsh Labour Party election manifesto in 2011 and formed part of the first suite of primary legislation to be introduced in Wales (under additional devolution of powers granted following a referendum in March 2011). The specific 2011 manifesto commitment was to legislate to make sustainable development the central organizing principle for the public sector (to replace the existing general duty which applied only to the Welsh Government) and to create a statutory Sustainable Development commissioner (to replace the existing non-statutory post in Wales, created following the UK's abolition of the UK Sustainable Development Commission in 2011).

Translating this general concept into a legislative form in a new parliamentary term and with new ministers fell initially to the very small team within my Directorate, working with drafting lawyers. As we came to draw up the proposals that became the Welsh Well-being Act, there was an opportunity to look around to see what progress others had made in the legal embedding of sustainable development. Examples were few. There were a number of general duties and additional constitutional sentences, such as the reference inserted in the European Union's Treaty, but they appeared to make sustainable development another thing to which to have regard rather than a central organizing principle. A major constitutional repositioning like that of Bolivia was off the table in UK law, where there is no written constitution. There were strategies and plans and reports tied in the UN reporting system, but they felt conventional in their scope and impact on governance. The UN Sustainable Development Goals were under development in succession to the Millennium Development Goals and we kept a close eye on their progress, while being wary of their scale and level of detail for their relevance to our goals of establishing new values. The Quebec 2006 Act was interesting – with 16 principles of sustainable development, a commissioner within the audit function and departmental plans – but it used a very conventional strategy and action plan approach not dissimilar to the original Welsh schemes (Happaerts, 2012). The Hungarian Ombudsman for Future Generations appeared something to explore further (though it was suspended in its original form in 2012 and succeeded by the Office of the Commissioner for Fundamental Rights). Estonia had published its Sustainable Development Act in 1995, and had a related protection in its constitution, but the legislation was very focused on the regulatory management of natural resources. In the end, it was the academic literature on transformatory governance for sustainable development which looked closest to what we were seeking. This also tapped into the democratizing spirit of the Welsh Government's origins.

In the opening public consultation on the proposal for the Well-being Act (WG, 2012a), and subsequently through its legal passage, the Act was cast expressly as setting principles for governing for sustainable development rather than addressing specific sectoral challenges or targets. The original consultations set what was to remain the fundamental structure of the Act – a general duty towards sustainable development reinforced with operational principles and broad directional goals. The opening consultation applied the 4Es behavioural change model (enable, engage, exemplify, encourage) which had recently been adopted by the UK government for steering *societal* change. Here, though, it was turned to address the question of what was holding back the *system of governance* from pursuing sustainability. A series of local workshops were held by my team to socialize the idea with the bodies that would be impacted by the act and to seek their feedback. Alongside this, the Sustainable Development Commissioner initiated a wider public engagement to help establish a societal vision for the Act. Dubbed 'The Wales We Want', this drew on the UN's 'The World We Want', working with the Welsh Sustainable Development NGO, Cynnal Cymru-Sustain Wales. The Commissioner also hosted a visit by an international group of fellow sustainability and future generations commissioner to inform the scope of the new role.

Legally binding goals

The original proposition was that sustainable development goals would be updated for each government term, not unlike the schemes under Wales' previous general legal duty. This would have continued to tie the approach directly to the government of the day, setting sustainable development as a political choice under the authority of the ballot box rather than as a (quasi-constitutional) context within which governance must operate. Judging by the experience of the schemes this might also have had the effect of moving them from expressions of purpose to something closer to shorter-term priorities. Following civil and parliamentary criticism that the goals should not be tied to the government of the day but should express universal civic values for sustainable development, Cabinet agreed to place the goals on the face of the primary legislation in perhaps the most significant shift in its early development. A process of civil society engagement was undertaken by officials, including a consultative group of NGOs, to fashion an agreed set of six equal narrative goals towards which public bodies should strive both individually and collectively. A further international goal was added during the passage of the legislation, at the request of international NGOs, bringing the total number of narrative goals to seven.

From sustainable development to well-being

The most notable public change through the development of the Act was a move from the working title of Sustainable Development Bill to Well-being of Future Generations. Responsibility for the legislation passed through four differing ministerial portfolios, moving from environmental to social departments and then back again. Future Generations reflected the Brundtland notion of intergenerational equity expressed in the report's guiding mantra – meeting the needs of the present without compromising the ability of future generations to meet their own needs. It also reflected contemporary interest in future generations commissioners (focused on representing and defending the voice of the young and unborn, regarded as a major gap (alongside the absent voice of the non-human world) within decision-making in representative democracy). The use of well-being picked up on the reference in the last Sustainable Development Scheme to the fashionable (utilitarian) concept that was part of contemporary UK political dialogue under the Cameron administration (2010–16). The recollection of interviewees was that the term emerged in discussion with the drafting lawyers as well-being was already established in law in respect of the general powers of local government. The title of the Commissioner became Future Generations alongside the changes. The new nomenclature was seen politically to address the perception of sustainable development as being an essentially environmental agenda.

New public bodies and plans

The process of developing the legislation also saw the late addition by the then Local Government Minister of statutory local Public Service Boards (replacing an existing informal structures of local authority-based inter-agency collaboration dubbed Local Service Boards). This addition placed an approach which had begun as a service delivery improvement initiative within the context for change provided by the Act. This was linked to the overall purpose of the Act through requirements for the Boards to produce local well-being plans. These replaced existing separate sectoral plans to allow for greater place-based connection and discretion, as well as a bureaucratic rationalization. This was in addition to the duties placed by the Act on each individual public body.

Scope of the Act

The final Well-being Act applies to all significant public bodies and local governments in Wales (a total of 44 bodies at the time of its publication) and is binding on the Welsh Government itself. The Act combines five behavioural principles for governance with seven broad, linked, narrative outcome goals. These behaviours and goals are underpinned by the Public Service Board area-based collaborative governance structures, spatial and institutional planning duties, and the statutory Future Generations Commissioner. The Act was accompanied by parallel changes to the purpose and institutional arrangements for environmental governance which were introduced in the Environment (Wales) Act 2016 and a partial refresh of land use planning legislation in the Planning (Wales) Act 2015.

Considering the Act as non-domination

The Act was expressly intended as a means of governing *for* sustainable development, fulfilling the commitment to give a statutory footing to making sustainable development the central organizing principle. This was articulated as follows in the initial consultation in May 2012:

> We want organisations to think about the implications of their work on long-term wellbeing. We want them to take into account the social, economic and environmental impacts before making a decision, but we do not want to specify in legislation that any particular outcome should be the result. We want to see organisations embed this way of thinking, and to be transparent about how they make these decisions, so that we start now to build better places. (WG, 2012a)

The Act can therefore be firmly positioned as addressing the Brundtland call of setting a new governance ethic of sustainable development and providing a counterweight to existing norms and practice. The Act and its accompanying legislation show a number of the characteristics that link its expression of governing for sustainable development to civic republican non-domination and to an ecological model of governance.

New express purpose: the narrative well-being goals

The seven narrative goals of the Act for public bodies are set out in Box 4.1. The goals are striking in setting express guiding values for the aims of public service. This moves a working definition of sustainable development from

---

Box 4.1: Well-being of Future Generations (Wales) Act 2015 goals (section 4)

In this Act, 'sustainable development' means the process of improving the economic, social, environmental and cultural well-being of Wales by taking action, in accordance with the sustainable development principle (see section 5), aimed at achieving the well-being goals (see section 4).

The goals:

1) An innovative, productive and low carbon society which recognizes the limits of the global environment and therefore uses resources efficiently and proportionately (including acting on climate change); and which develops a skilled and well-educated population in an economy which generates wealth and provides employment opportunities, allowing people to take advantage of the wealth generated through securing decent work.

2) A nation which maintains and enhances a biodiverse natural environment with healthy functioning ecosystems that support social, economic and ecological resilience and the capacity to adapt to change (for example climate change).
3) A society in which people's physical and mental well-being is maximized and in which choices and behaviours that benefit future health are understood.
4) A society that enables people to fulfil their potential no matter what their background or circumstances (including their socio-economic background and circumstances).
5) Attractive, viable, safe and well-connected communities.
6) A society that promotes and protects culture, heritage and the Welsh language, and which encourages people to participate in the arts, and sports and recreation.
7) A nation which, when doing anything to improve the economic, social, environmental and cultural well-being of Wales, takes account of whether doing such a thing may make a positive contribution to global well-being.

---

a debated political issue to a defined functional bureaucratic one. Both the legal goals and behaviours of the Act were put in framed posters throughout the Welsh Government bureaucratic estate and promoted with staff. Despite the ambiguity of some of the drafting, the goals replace the unstated values behind the 'neutrality' of public service. They provided express values for bureaucracy to measure its neutrality for the first time in place of the existing neutrality of technocratic efficiency. The Act thus reduces the scope for tacit assumptions about what is right and normal, assumptions that tend to reinforce existing power structures. This was seen by the Welsh interview discussants as providing a 'missing frame' for bureaucratic work.

There was a recognition among the discussant practitioners in Wales that the Act was concerned with changing long-established values and behaviours and that this was an issue for the long-haul. To date (at the 2019 interview dates) they felt that the Act had begun to change the dialogue and the nature of debate, but this was difficult to measure in conventional ways and there was no counterfactual with which to compare the new position. Several talked of needing at least ten years to understand the impact.

The establishment of the new legal frameworks (and the accompanying institutions) was seen as a major success in itself by practitioners. The frameworks had provided the visible weight needed to shake traditional bureaucratic and political approaches. The Act was widely viewed as an opportunity to reconsider existing paths. As one former minister put it: "The Act is the permission to think differently."

The statutory guidance accompanying the Act clarifies that all goals must be considered together and equally, and that all are relevant, whatever the work topic area. So, as well as setting express values to which bureaucracy should work, the legal approach counters the bounded, sectoralized nature of existing bureaucracy that permits one sector or interest to dominate others. This recalls Brundtland's call to ensure ministries that cause environmental harm are responsible for that impact. This is underlined in the accompanying statutory behaviours of collaboration and integration under the Act.

Each legislative goal aims to capture what is different about the purpose of governing for sustainable development in its broad topic area. While the intention is that the goals are taken in the round, it is interesting to deconstruct the language of the individual goals. This shows an element of their drafting by committee but is perhaps most useful to see what is included and what is omitted as they relate to aspects of domination. For fun, I've given each a notional score out of five for transformatory quality. Overall, the drafting falls somewhere in the mid-ground between the conventional and the transformative but, even in its ambiguity, contributes to the Act's permission to think differently.

Goal 1 - the 'economy' goal — is noted for the absence of loaded words like growth, competitiveness, infrastructure, industry, trade or markets, all usually associated with legitimizing an economic dominance. It also begins with the term society. In referencing global environmental limits, and in the oblique reference to one planet living in using resources proportionately, the goal appears to seek to counter the dominance of economic activity over the environment. In contrast, the references to innovation, productivity, low carbon, a skilled and well-educated population, wealth creation and decent jobs map directly on to an ecological modernization or green new deal narrative as a response to environmental limits rather than to the potential alternative 'prosperity without growth' narrative. Beyond the reference to decent work, there are also no signs of social concerns here. The assumption appears to be that wealth and jobs, subject to the other goals and within global environmental limits, equal a decent society. (Transformatory factor 2/5)

Goal 2 – the 'environmental' goal – positions itself in a systemic view of the environment and nature and their relationship to economy and society rather than a dominating 'othering' of nature. It links increased biodiversity to healthy functioning ecosystems and their contribution to social, economic and environmental resilience and adaptation. It does not refer to conservation or protections, nor does it use the economic language of the ecological modernization narrative such as ecosystem services, natural capital or nature-based solutions. (Transformatory factor 4/5)

Goal 3 – the 'health' goal – embraces both physical and mental well-being rather than using the word health and focuses on public health 'wellness' issues rather than the treatment services which are the usual focus of politics. The references to choice and behaviours most likely sets this goal within a psychological rather the sociological frame, pointing to views of personal choice and responsibility rather than underlying societal factors affecting health. (Transformatory factor 2/5)

Goal 4 – the 'equality' goal – has a focus on enabling all to fulfil their potential, specifically referencing the barriers presented by socio-economic circumstances. This is certainly governance where freedom is non-domination rather than freedom as non-interference. Unlike most other goals, however, it does not offer any indication of how this is to be achieved. (Transformatory factor 4/5)

Goal 5 – the community goal – is open to interpretation. If 'well connected' means socially connected rather than transport connected, it is firmly in a space of civic dialogue and inclusion. It may suggest community is related to the quality and strength of place – the reterritorialization supported in the new institutional structures of the Act. Alternatively, the word 'attractive' may conjure up the economic dominance of gentrification and 'viable' may reference the economic view of necessary agglomeration. (Transformatory factor 2.5/5)

Goal 6 – the cultural goal – is a conventional expression of the roles of a culture department – covering promoting and protecting culture, heritage, and participation in arts and sports. There is no additional explanation of why or who/what is to benefit, though the absence of a reference to excellence in arts and sport suggests inclusion. The distinctive non-domination element is the promotion of the Welsh language (a Celtic language spoken by some 25 per cent of the population). (Transformatory factor 2/5)

Goal 7 – the (late added) international goal – conditions all work on well-being in Wales to consider the positive contribution action in Wales might make to global well-being. This non-domination over other nations aligns with the multilateral call of the Brundtland introduction and Pettit's later writing on republicanism (Pettit, 2014). (The slightly odd language reflects the lack of international powers of the Welsh Government.) (Transformatory factor 4/5)

Overall, the Well-being Act goals present a focus on inclusion, diversity and community connections and eschew a conventional language of political economy. While they do not present a fully coherent viewpoint, the language has strong emancipatory and egalitarian aspects.

The accompanying Environment Act set out a position on nature which includes both a moral imperative (referring to the intrinsic worth of nature) and a utilitarian, anthropocentric perspective (of the benefits the natural world provides humankind). It links species protection to wider ecosystem health rather than direct conservation. Its viewpoint sits closer to the perspective of complex interactive social-ecological systems than to a classical liberal market or conservative traditionalist one. Like the Well-being Act, it consciously makes no reference to the market terms of (payments for) ecosystems services nor to economic conceptions such as natural capital.

Changing bureaucratic practice: the sustainable development principle and behaviours

Alongside the goals' redefinition of the purpose of governing, the sustainable development principle redefines the way in which governance should operate, its governance and bureaucratic practice. It set out five 'ways of working' drawn from the sense of 'governing *for* sustainable development'. They sit in the Act under the Brundtland mantra of meeting needs and mirror the asks of the Brundtland Report's introduction. They state that the approach to governance should be long-term, preventative, integrated, collaborative and involving of diverse interests (Box 4.2).

Box 4.2: Well-being of Future Generations (Wales) Act 2015 principle (section 5)

The sustainable development principle

(1) In this Act, any reference to a public body doing something 'in accordance with the sustainable development principle' means that the body must act in a manner which seeks to ensure that the needs of the present are met without compromising the ability of future generations to meet their own needs.

(2) In order to act in that manner, a public body must take account of the following things:

    (a) the importance of balancing short-term needs with the need to safeguard the ability to meet long-term needs, especially where things done to meet short-term needs may have detrimental long-term effect;

    (b) the need to take an integrated approach, by considering how:

        (i) the body's well-being objectives may impact upon each of the well-being goals;

        (ii) the body's well-being objectives impact upon each other or upon other public bodies' objectives, in particular where steps taken by the body may contribute to meeting one objective but may be detrimental to meeting another;

    (c) the importance of involving other persons with an interest in achieving the well-being goals and of ensuring those persons reflect the diversity of the population of (i) Wales (where the body exercises functions in relation to the whole of Wales), or (ii) the part of Wales in relation to which the body exercises functions;

(d) how acting in collaboration with any other person (or how different parts of the body acting together) could assist the body to meet its well-being objectives, or assist another body to meet its objectives;

(e) how deploying resources to prevent problems occurring or getting worse may contribute to meeting the body's well-being objectives, or another body's objectives.

Despite somewhat cumbersome drafting, the five ways of working directly challenge the short-termism, technocracy and bounded rationality of bureaucracy's inherited norms. They fit well with a view of governance as pursuing non-domination through plural dialogue and collaboration, rather than dominance through competition and the exercise of knowledge-power. They emphasize the importance of civil society engagement in governance but also of the focus for governance on meeting on long-term needs, not allowing the present to dominate the future.

The language of the Act as a whole, being an Act, is conventional and somewhat staid. The behaviours use language largely drawn from conventional consultation and co-ordination except for the emphasis placed on diversity. The emphasis on having to have something legally defined on which to hang actions is clear (and very clunky) – in this case it is the published well-being objectives of the bodies.

The use of the expression of 'balancing' at (2) (a) recalls weak not strong forms of sustainability. There is no application here of fashionable terms such as co-production as used in policy work by the Welsh Government which could give a clearer steer as to what is expected by way of process. The very constrained text on involvement, limited to interest in the goals, is particularly weak from the perspective of the potential for domination in the way in which bodies may choose to engage their populations.

New institutional arrangements

The Act introduced a range of new institutions associated with aspects of minimizing domination

Public Service Boards

To support the local, collaborative and integrative ways of working, the Act gave a legal basis to local Public Service Boards, formal boards of representatives of mandated public bodies operating in a given area, together with locally determined representatives of civil society. The Boards are charged with developing and keeping up to date a well-being plan for their area to inform their own and others' work.

Interview discussants felt that the Public Service Boards had generally begun to step up to the opportunity of considering the needs of their areas in the round. The thematic peer learning undertaken by local government officials as part of the support of the Act's implementation had been positive and there were a number of collaborative initiatives on both services and identifying issues and questions. The first round of local statutory well-being plans had been a mixed bag in the time available but had interesting examples of imaginative work.

Future Generations Commissioner

The Well-being Act established a Commissioner for Future Generations with a seven-year term of appointment in order to extend beyond the normal political cycle. The role was intended primarily as one to support public bodies in pursuing and understanding their functions under the Act – one of co-learning and dialogue – with a particular focus on the intergenerational aspect of governing for sustainable development. The Commissioner is also charged with a forward-looking report on future generations. Additional powers and duties were added during the passage of the Act to shift the role to one with more perceived teeth in ensuring delivery of the Act, taking a more adversarial stance compared with the Act's aim of building common purpose.

The establishment of the Future Generations Commissioner seeks to reflect the interest of the unrepresented – in this case literally the unborn. This proxy representation has been advocated to give voice to the voiceless, including nature, from a green republican perspective (Eckersley, 2004), addressing the limitations of dialogue as a means of developing a civic understanding which can embrace the interest of nature or of people in the future. Governments have also sought to give greater voice to younger people in the existing democratic process, most notably by lowering of the voting age, as the Welsh Senedd itself did by reducing the voting age to 16 for the 2021 elections.

The idea of the Commissioner drew on the experience of those countries which have established Sustainable Development, Wellbeing or Future Generations Ombudsman, Commissioners or Auditors of varying roles and forms in order to represent the interest of the future. These roles include challenging or auditing governmental practice or decision-making, reporting publicly on trends, and promoting awareness and good practice (Anderson, 2018). Such approaches in themselves provide an institutional champion without otherwise changing the nature of the bureaucratic or governance model. In providing a voice and legitimacy for future generations or wider issues of sustainable development across government, Commissioners may make these a stronger factor in decision-making. However, in a conventional inter-agency competition view of institutional governance, there is always the risk of Commissioners being drawn into the adversarial style of competitive democracy rather than helping to widen civic dialogue.

The Environment Act and Natural Resources Wales

Natural Resources Wales (NRW) was established shortly before the passage of the two Welsh Acts (using order making powers provided under UK legislation). It brought together the existing Forestry, Environmental Regulation and Management, and Countryside and Nature functions in Wales into a new single agency charged with the sustainable management of natural resources. The Environment (Wales) Act 2016 (the Environment Act) concluded the process of the new body's establishment by mandating NRW to produce area statements (in an accidental nod to Foucault), setting out the natural resource issues and opportunities in different parts of Wales. These are for information rather than regulatory but public bodies must have regard to these statements in conducting their work and in land use planning. NRW also has a duty to produce and update a statement on the state of natural resources in Wales to which the Welsh Government must have regard in producing its statutory strategy for natural resources. The second State of Natural Resources Report under this duty was issued in December 2020 (NRW, 2020). Natural Resources Wales is the only public agency represented on all the Public Service Boards.

The names used for the body capture conflicting narrative views of nature. The English language title *Natural Resources Wales* suggests a utilitarian or natural capital viewpoint reflecting nationalism and classical liberalism. Its Welsh title, however, *Cyfoeth Naturiol Cymru* (the natural wealth or riches of Wales), conveys a more cultural (nationalist) connotation. The consultation documents that led to the body's creation and to the Environment Act, in contrast, used the term *A Living Wales*, taking language from an ecological standpoint.

New processes of non-domination

The specific duties through which the Act is operationalized may be considered prosaic. They set what one academic colleague at a seminar on the Act called "surprisingly conventional" requirements for boards, plans, reports, corporate planning, statements and consultation. This recalls Philip Pettit's 'gas and works board' approach to republicanism where the goal is for the design of the ordinary processes of governance to foreground the desired changes rather than reinforce existing assumptions.

Territory and reterritorialization

The Acts place a strong emphasis on place-based levels of governance and operation. Place-based plans, statements and bodies are central to thier conception. In doing this they embrace sustainability as a locally specific, reflexive concept and promote a civic republican view of distributed governance and subsidiarity.

The Environment Act includes a requirement for land use planning to have regard to the statutory area statements made by NRW. In parallel to the passage of the Acts, new Welsh planning legislation (the Planning (Wales) Act 2015) made sustainable development the goal of planning policy. Welsh planning guidance was then rewritten to emphasize its role in sustainable place making. How and the extent to which this has yet been reflected is discussed later in the chapter.

Audit discipline

The Act added powers to the role of the existing Auditor General to enable examination of public bodies against the Act rather than restrict audit to the existing propriety and value for money focus of the external audit role.

From control and targets to uncertainty and reflexivity: flexible bureaucracy

No targets or specific outcomes were set in the Act despite pressure for them from environmental lobbies and the Assembly. As the then responsible minister, Carl Sargeant, stated in Committee, invoking the Brundtland idea of the journey:

> '[W]e will resist the process about targets and exactly what that public authority should achieve and in what time. This is a journey and is about taking people from the place where they are now – and we are all at very different positions in the public sector – to a better place and a better Wales.' (National Assembly, 2014, 32)

The Act sustains a focus on setting governance purpose and behaviours rather than determining and managing their specific outputs. Aspects of a managerialist perspective are largely absent from the legislation. Not only does the Act not set targets for specific activities, nor does it set priorities for others, except in so far as these might flow from the required National Policy Statement under the Environment Act. The Environment Act provides considerable discretion about how the duties are taken forward in local contexts and the accountabilities of the public bodies are limited to the publication of the various statements and plans under the Act. Except for some of the words in the economy goal, there is little language of modernism or managerialism in the Act. The managerialist accountabilities which do appear in the Act, such as milestones and reporting requirements, and scrutiny powers of the Commissioner were principally added through Welsh parliamentary input in the passage of the Bill.

License to act differently

Discussants felt that the Acts had generated a range of new initiatives across public bodies and civil society, such as work on low impact housing undertaken by housing associations. Initiatives of place-based and landscape-scale working were prominent. These included the work of the Valleys Task Force in collaborative and participative development of the concept of the Valleys Regional Park in South-East Wales; NRW's pilot work on area statements, such the detailed work of the Swansea Bay area pilot that drew in local people and exposed inequalities of access to nature and water in the area; and NRW's multifunctional investment in forestry in the Llynfi Valley. The two Acts had generated independent work at landscape scale. Welsh Water-Dwr Cymru's megacatchment initiative brought together landholders and public bodies in the Brecon Beacons National Park to consider the management of the area to multiple objectives through bottom-up, collaborative working. The social enterprise led Project Skyline in the South Wales Valleys took an innovative approach to working with communities to reimagine their relationship to their landscape and ultimately to empower them by seeking to move that landscape into long-term community management or ownership.

Official discussants felt that the Acts had strengthened place as a factor in both policy and analysis: the work in Wales on the distributional impact of Brexit had, for example, included spatial as well as sectoral implications. Politicians had begun to build narratives around the Act. The new First Minister, Mark Drakeford, had placed the Act at the centre of his policy agenda and in presentations to staff. The programme for government had included the statement of objectives under the Act within its pages. The decision not to proceed with the M4 motorway proposals, while not narratively linked to the Act, was seen as a litmus test of the application of the Act's values.

Some public bodies had championed the Act. The newly established Transport for Wales, the oversight body for rail operation and investment, was seen as a leading example of embedding the values and goals. The existing transport assessment model had specifically been updated to reflect the Act. NRW had made a positive contribution to the debate in the Public Service Boards as the only public body which was represented on each one. The example of well-being frameworks was also adopted by non-governmental entities: my Institute supported work by the Canal & River Trust to build a well-being framework to evaluate and improve their own impacts (Canal & River Trust, 2017).

The Welsh Government had developed internal change programmes reconsidering its performance management, leadership development and behaviours. The Act had given stimulus to develop different ways of working, such as the example of an early departmental behaviours statement in Appendix 2. Appendix 3 contains the submission by the Permanent Secretary (lead public administrator) of the Welsh Government made to the formal review of barriers to progress on the Well-being Act undertaken by the Welsh Senate Public Accounts Committee. I include this in full as a rare example of a public document in this field written from a bureaucratic rather than political perspective. It is notable for its understanding of the degree of change necessary to practice, albeit flavoured with some managerialism:

> I recognise that the Act is fundamentally about changing behaviours and how decisions are made. The kind of sustained behaviour change expected by the legislation and sustainable development agenda takes time, and requires continual improvements in how we lead; how we learn; how we perform; and, how we work. (Welsh Parliament, 2021a)

In March 2021, the Welsh Senedd Public Accounts Committee published its report – *Delivering for Future Generations: The Story So Far* (Welsh Parliament, 2021b) drawing on evidence from 97 public bodies. The foreword states:

> Although few people disagreed with what the Well-being of Future Generations (Wales) Bill set out to achieve when it was introduced to the National Assembly for Wales in 2014, many were sceptical about whether it was possible to implement sustainable development via legislation. Many still are. Nevertheless, as we prepare to publish this report, scepticism is no longer good enough. We as a Senedd, and as a country, have a collective responsibility to reshape public services in Wales for the better. We must learn lessons from how we have responded to Covid-19 and use this opportunity to shape a better future for generations to come. Implementing the principles of the Well-being of Future Generations (Wales) Act 2015 is a good place to start. (Nick Ramsay MS, chair PAC). (Welsh Parliament, 2021b, 5)

What is missing from the Act?

The Act established new structures, new processes and set out new narratives for the purpose of bureaucratic endeavour and its tools. It was conceived as an encouragement to explore reflexively new way of working. It does not therefore place a large amount of legal detail into what should occur.

The Act did not create new rights exercisable by individuals or private entities. Its focus is on establishing new common behaviours and goals of public administration. In a constitutional context, expression of rights for future generations, rights for nature and the environment and social rights might be expected. These are instead covered as governance goals to be applied in setting strategic direction.

The Act has some of the characteristics of constitutional law, expressing overall values, behaviours and creating institutional structures and duties. However, there is no provision for a written constitution in UK legislation, so any other legislation of the Parliament could overrule or amend the Well-being Act by simple majority. This makes the Act vulnerable both to inconsistencies of future legislation and the use and interpretation of past legislation.

The potential weakest facet of the Act from a civic republican perspective is the absence of the definition in detail of alternative processes of governance such for public engagement or decision-making. Its only bite in this area is indirectly through the requirement on each body to set out how it is implementing the Act and to set short-term objectives for this, and in the guidance and peer learning support offered to bodies. There are no legally required single corporate planning processes for public bodies in Wales to which the legislation could attach. Although there is a clear tension between the desire for reflexive new behaviours and the making of detailed process requirements, the present framing means that the Act gives space for quixotic or relatively arbitrary political decisions with the only route of challenge available being the costly and difficult one of judicial review of a decision.

There is no requirement on how different forms of decision or strategy development should in detail apply the ways of working and values. This is particularly of concern given the limited and simplistic requirements for public consultation in existing law and the heavy focus on economic rationale and measurement used in existing decision-making processes and regulation. This falls short of the need for binding and transparent legal process on public policy decisions – governance by the rule of law. As one senior official, in an echo of Pettit's civic republican view, said:

> 'If you are going to govern for sustainable development, you need things that are going to operate at the heart of that system and speak to that system ... but you can't just have something overarching. You need to bring it down to all the bits of delivery. You need to amend associated law and processes.'

The Act did not replace or significantly amend existing legislation. It therefore sits as a general call to an alternative form of governing while existing law continues to require traditional processes and to focus on specific bounded responsibilities. This is a particular problem in UK law where more specific provisions always override the more general. The Act can therefore be viewed as unfinished business from the perspective of providing coherent alternative rule of law in respect of bureaucratic practice and decision-making.

The Act has provided some limited avenues for contestation. Where there are existing legal processes of decision such as in infrastructure proposals, challenge based on the failure to apply the aims of the Act can be made at public enquiry (as they were with the M4 motorway proposal, seen as a first test of whether the Act had teeth). It is also open to the Future Generations Commissioner to make formal representations and the Auditor General may choose to investigate a decision using powers under the Act. Internally to the Welsh Government, administrative procedures put in place to reflect the Act require submissions and Cabinet papers to state what impact the proposal has in relation to the Act. While these are not made public in advance, discussants stated that Cabinet papers had been challenged by ministers due to the lack of reflection of the goals. The Act is also being used by Senate Committees in their scrutiny role.

The Act does not directly bind budget setting, procurement or grant making. The Public Accounts Committee report on five years of implementation (Welsh Parliament, 2021b) focuses heavily on budgeting, calling for more resources for the Commissioner's office (which has had to be met to date within my old department's existing budget), funding to support Public Service Boards, support for dissemination and, more structurally, for a move to longer-term funding/planning cycles for public bodies. Given procurement and grants are the principal forms of societal steering used by the Welsh Government, as in many other governments worldwide, these feel an important omission from the Act. There was a call for, and internal discussion of, including procurement in the Act but proposals then being considered for separate procurement legislation meant this was omitted from the final provisions. In practice, some changes to grant giving terms have been made to reflect the legislation – notably additional conditions on economic development grants (see later in this chapter). Early experimentation in less directive use of grants to third parties and local government has been patchy in the absence of a specific legal requirement for a different approach (see case examples in Chapter 3). Grant giving remains a centralist tool which is prey to concerns of centralism, clientelism and arbitrary decision.

The one area completely untouched by the Act, except indirectly in the first goal, is the operation of the economy and the role of business. This reflects the focus of the Act on public decision-making. There has been no related legislation in the economic development field. The Welsh Government's action with businesses operates through grant making and infrastructure funding. The Welsh Government has limited powers of business regulation and taxation. These are largely reserved to the UK government.

The Act does not expressly talk of a role in strengthening civic engagement and understanding and, in its legal drafting, does not use language associated with such interests. Effective delivery of the Act was, however, seen by discussants in that context, as one discussant noted: "If we had done the Act 30 years ago, we wouldn't have this disaffection."

The Act and competing narratives

Taking Foucault's focus on the power of narratives and the significance of statements in knowledge-power, it is perhaps not surprising that the process of the Act and its subsequent implementation can be seen as a competition of language reflecting other values. These narratives are worth exploring as they give a good sense of the pitfalls which attempts at transformative change need to address.

Control and targetry versus common purpose and reflexive transformation

The Act was criticized during its parliamentary passage for its unusual focus on changing the ethos of public bureaucracy to create an enabling framework for sustainable development rather than directing specific public policy actions (Wallace, 2018). The criticism came largely from environmental groups and was based on a managerialist framing of the legislation which expected legally binding targets and milestones on specific topics. This criticism led to the parliamentary amendments which inserted more conventional metrics into the Act around milestones and gave the Commissioner stronger directive powers.

The NGOs who organized to lobby on the Act initially advocated a simple declaratory approach to the Act with accompanying sanctions and published their own four-page legislation which was used as a rod to beat the process- and values-heavy government proposal. The focus of challenge was very much on governing *of* rather than *for* sustainable development. There was little interest in changing the wider nature of governance to support sustainable outcomes. The overall focus of critique was on the desire for centralized command and control and specific actions and targets, with little interest in participative, change-based or place-based governance. Parties also joined to criticize the Act as meaningless 'motherhood and apple pie' that would be burdensome to undertake and have no practical impact because it failed to specify precise outputs. Based on this 'bureaucratic critique', the nationalist party Plaid Cymru attempted to sabotage the Act in Committee by voting for the deletion of large sections but not then supporting their replacement with the text proposed in response to the Committee's earlier comments. In contrast to previous votes under the former sustainable development scheme, which were generally passed unanimously, the Act passed with a bare majority. Perhaps this was a sign that the new legislation had challenged governance norms in a way that the gentler sustainable development schemes had not.

In response to threats from the environmental NGOs to withdraw support for the Well-being Act if there were no specific commitments on climate change action, an additional section was added very late in the drafting of the Environment Act introducing requirements for setting carbon budgets. The NGO group subsequently took out a newspaper advertisement encouraging members to support the Well-being Bill at its final stage.

The Confederation of British Industry argued that the Act constituted big government which would undermine economic growth. Criticism continues of the Public Service Boards as another layer in what is perceived in Wales as a crowded multilevel system of governance, with early pressure from local government to move to a regional tier of co-operation seen in the fields of economy and health. Such managerialist rationalization would undermine the local reflexivity intended in the Act.

Sectoralism versus systemic change

The sustainability agenda of the Act chiefly attracted environmental lobbying. There were some attempts to use the Act by other lobby groups which were passed over to other legislative vehicles (for example an attempt to give recognition to the role of carers). Despite work by the Sustainable Development Commissioner to engage public debate through *The Wales We Want* exercise, it was evident that the conventional lobbying by political interest groups did not offer advocacy for systemic change. Civil society organization and methods mirrored the divided and competitive structures of bureaucratic governance.

Representative politics: the shock of the old

Officials prepared diligently for the implications of the Act ahead of the first new Welsh Government term following the Bill's passage. Working groups were set up across departments, with a younger participant group than usual, to consider how they could focus together on some of the big issues rather than stay in their siloes. Interesting ideas on issues that touched on drivers of inequality and environmental degradation were considered. Officials looked forward to the opportunities to explore these with the incoming administration. Instead, they were confronted with traditional politics, with the focus on implementing the newly elected government's manifesto in the new programme for government, rather than considering the strategic implications of the new legislation as judged by bureaucrats. This caused a palpable shock to a bureaucratic system which had thought it had a legal mandate. It prompted an early back-pedalling on referencing the Act and led to quite a few colleagues, notably in the economy department, expressing the view that ministers hadn't really intended or understood the legislation.

Purpose and the pervasive language of political economy

The Act appeared during a continued focus on jobs and growth and public service improvement. The initial programme for government following the Act's passage, *Taking Wales Forward* (WG, 2016), stated: 'The Welsh Government's relentless focus will be on driving improvement in our economy and public services, which are together the bedrock of people's daily lives.' The final version of the programme took the title *Prosperity for All* (WG, 2017a), certainly an accidental echo of a think tank piece of two years previously with a focus on restoring faith in capitalism (Montgomery, 2015). The Welsh Government also welcomed UK government borrowing approval to expand the M4 motorway in South Wales and engaged with the UK government's City Deal offers which promoted regional economic competitiveness based on the agglomeration model and did not include the Act as a contextual requirement.

The first economic action plan issued under the new government (WG, 2017b) revealed the tension between existing practice and new ideas. In contrast to the Well-being goals, the introduction used modernist narrative language: innovative, dynamic, world-class, growth, competitiveness and commercial exploitation of research. The strategy's reflection of the Act showed a wealth of adjectivalism – 'sustainable, inclusive growth' and 'low carbon productivity'. The paper made specific changes, however, to the operation of future inward investment programmes and government support to reflect the Act. The new Economic Contract with businesses sought a commitment from businesses seeking investment funding to contribute formally to one of the Act's economic sub-goals – fair work, addressing climate change, skills, learning and health in the workplace, alongside traditional requirements for growth, innovation, export potential, R&D and high skills. The Strategy also introduced a commitment to foster the foundational economy alongside its traditional pursuit of encouraging mobile investment in the traded economy and committed to reflect spatial variation and address areas of low economic activity, was linked to the Well-being Act sub-goal of decent, local jobs. This largely involved reconfiguring of the Economic Departments teams to feature three regional directorates, although with no linkage to the Act's Public Service Board structures. Except for the option of health promotion in the new Economic Contract and the structural reflection of geographic diversity, reflections of the Act's goals in the document were restricted to the single economic goal. This approach of gravitating to the 'nearest' goal can be seen in other areas, despite the statutory guidance to the Act saying that all goals should be considered equally.

The language of economic efficiency also found its way into the implementation of the Environment Act. Natural Resources Wales commissioned research work on environmental capital in Wales and the first Natural Resource Policy statement of the Welsh Government focused on ecosystem services and set economic efficiency objectives (linked to *Prosperity for All* (WG, 2017a)) of supporting successful, sustainable communities; promoting green growth and innovation to create sustainable jobs; supporting a more resource efficient economy; and maintaining healthy, active and connected communities (WG, 2017c).

Territory and planning

The Welsh Government undertook a formal review of its planning guidance following the passage of the Well-being Act and Planning Act. The resulting revised Planning Policy Wales (WG, 2018) brings out similar tensions between the view of existing planning policy and sustainable development and is in many ways a rebadging of existing approaches. The document begins with the broad commitment to sustainable development linked to the requirements of the Well-being Act and goes on to set 'achieving well-being through placemaking' as its opening goal. This is then divided into four themes – strategic and spatial choices, active and social places, distinctive and natural places, and productive and enterprising – with reference to the Well-being Act goals and associated linking text. Within this framework, however, it rolls forward the existing focus of predict and provide provision for major housing, commercial, leisure and business developments, including the forward availability of land and technical tests of need. The Act also introduced two provisions based on English approaches: a new National Development Framework replacing the Spatial Plan (to fit with the UK National Infrastructure Planning process for major development) and the possibility of strategic development plans crossing local authority boundaries.

Looking elsewhere: other legal innovations in sustainability governance

The British tradition is weak on the provision of rights and does not have experience of working with a written constitution. The scope of action in the Act was also limited by the Welsh Government's legal scope which does not extend to tools of the nation state – major taxation, regulation of finance and markets, major welfare provision and international trade and agreements. It was also limited by parliamentary and legal time and was unable to make comprehensive change to other regimes such as land use. The Welsh case thus lacks potential means of governing as non-domination which would be relevant to other legal traditions and to nation state and international institutions. This last section of the chapter considers international exemplars which fill out some of these gaps.

Rights and constitutional protections

As recommended by Brundtland, governments have created constitutional rights to enjoyment of a clean environment. Analysis of such provisions (Boyd, 2012) suggest they have been useful in strengthening legal provisions, providing legal redress and avoiding regression. Broad commitments to sustainable development have also been added to constitutions, most notably in the EU Treaty. The very broad framing of such provisions makes their direct impact unclear. They typically sit alongside competing narratives and goals leaving unresolved tensions. They are not accompanied by wider revisions to reflect the implications of the transformatory needs of governing for sustainable development.

More radically, constitutional and legal rights have been offered to nature itself or to natural entities. The best known of these are Ecuador and Bolivia's constitutions of 2008 and 2009, respectively, based on the concept of *buen vivir*, which gives ecosystems the right to exist, persist, maintain and regenerate. This provision has been both impactful and widely praised as a means of redressing the long-standing exploitative power balance between the human and the natural worlds (Kauffman and Martin, 2017). Courts and administrations have elsewhere extended rights to individual natural features: Indian courts recognized Himalayan glaciers and the Ganges and Yamuna rivers as 'legal persons' in 2017, enabling legal guardians to represent the waterways in court, while in New Zealand the Whanganui river was legally recognized as an ancestor. Such rights have the impact of widening the contestability of decisions regarding the domination of nature. The idea of providing nature with fundamental and inalienable rights has been picked up in local jursidictions such as growing numbers of resolutions by local governments in the United States to confer rights on the local landscape or watershed.

Engagement and participation

Latin America offers a study of benefits and potential pitfalls of participative and deliberative forms of governance, with their pioneering role in areas such as participatory budgeting. Innovation here has been focused more on democratization of governance than an express focus on governance for sustainable development. This has tested the prospects for achieving and sustaining genuine and egalitarian participation. Continuing clientelism, co-option and limited inclusion has limited its impact in moving towards creating the wider civic engagement and contestability that proponents sought (Montambeault, 2015). This mixed experience of participation requirements within existing power structures emphasizes the need for detailed legal forms and ethical values for participation and contestation that seek to establish a more level playing field, including potentially support for intermediary civic institutions.

Territory

In the Anglo-Saxon tradition different uses of land are covered by different legislation. As I have been known to say, in a nod to the opening line of Caesar's *Gallic Wars*, England and Wales are, since the Second World War, divided into four parts – respectively governed by the Forestry Acts, the Agriculture Acts, the Town and Country Planning Acts and the National Parks Acts. It was this type of division that New Zealand sought to address with its Resource Management Act 1991. This offered an early innovation in making the basis of all land use decisions the promotion of the sustainable management of land, replacing a large sweep of existing legislation in a comprehensive new framework. When I visited New Zealand on my study trip in in 1992, it was the main topic of conversation within the public administration. Speaking informally to one of the instigators of the Act a few years ago when they visited Wales, there was a sense that the original intentions had been lost along the way and amendments to the legislation over time had reduced its edge and clarity. In a recent assessment (Miller, 2011), the Act is seen as exposing the huge challenge of applying sustainable development principles in a contested area such as planning without commensurate changes to the wider governance framework. A 2020 Review Panel recommended replacing the Act with three new pieces of legislation focused on more targeted delivery of objectives – a Natural and Built Environment Act to define more precisely the nature of sustainable use of land, a Strategic Planning Act to integrate planning and funding, and a Managed Retreat and Climate Change Act to address this discrete challenge for a coastal nation (Resource Management Review Panel, 2020).

In France, the loi Voynet, of 1999, made sustainable development the purpose of territorial organization. The impact of the act has run into tension between differing models of development, as did the Welsh Spatial Plan before it. This is especially true in conflict between the growth pole economic agglomeration model of development and the alternative goal of territorial integrity with its desire for more even distribution of development

(Bertrand, 2005). This basic tension between distribution of benefit from development and the aim of maximizing its economic efficiency comes in addition to the more specific technical and social questions as to which detailed forms of development constitute sustainable approaches. Just as with other forms of bureaucratic decision, sustainable development as a general (and contested) concept would need itself to be translated to more specific values and actions if it is to steer the system of territorial planning consistently (Owens and Cowell, 2002).

The lessons of legislating for bureaucratic change

The legal approach to changing bureaucratic governance narratives and practice can have an impact in challenging and resetting the self-reproduction of the existing system and addressing the tension between civic and economic conceptions of how bureaucracy should function. The Welsh case and the international examples have demonstrated key elements of reform and how these can be understood in terms of both governing for sustainable development and civic republicanism. They have also shown the pressure of old ways of approaching governance. To be effective legislation needs to be comprehensive and bite on all aspects of bureaucratic endeavour. It also needs to walk the tightrope of being specific enough to have teeth on the process issues which matter without constraining the desired reflexivity and creativity for transformatory responses.

While the opening quotation to the chapter reminds us that destabilisation of the status quo is a good start, ultimately such comprehensive changes need to be able to attract and develop political, sectoral and civil society support and understanding to enable their continued reproduction. This includes (and requires) the effective empowerment of new more participative forms of governance. It may also mean fresh (potentially constitutional) expression for roles, values, rights and duties. Without these changes in organization and purpose, old practices and narratives can easily chip away at the legislative intent.

5

A new civic bureaucracy

> If we are to put in new boilers and to mend the fires which drive
> our government machinery, we must not leave the old wheels
> and joints and valves and bands to creek and buzz and clatter as
> best they may at bidding of new forces.
>
> Woodrow Wilson

Woodrow Wilson used a very mechanical metaphor for his call for fresh approaches to public administration at the close of the 19th century. This book calls instead for a socio-ecological expression of the tradition of civic republicanism as its pathway to transformatory change for the 21st century, one in which we move from a controlling bounded rationality to supporting a reflexive, place-based, discursive democracy that fosters a pan- or at least polyarchy of social and ecological reconnection and non-domination. The final chapter spells out the specific kind of changes and the likely legal underpinning needed for this new civic bureaucracy. Through them we may hope to achieve a new guiding purpose of reflexive, civic reconnections that can help to unlock the present system and address the democratic impasse that risks planetary health and threatens democracy itself.

The opening chapters explored the way in which dominant narratives of governance, bureaucracy and sustainable development have largely co-opted the potential emancipatory power of the original ethical call of the Brundtland Report. This has resulted in a failure to recognize or realize the transformatory implications for governance and public bureaucracy represented by the challenge posed by the concept of governing *for* sustainable development. Nevertheless, examining the competing narratives reminds us of the transformative potential that these alternatives represent and that they are closely related to the civic republican tradition of seeing the role of governance as a civic force to mitigate domination by or of others – a mitigation which is to be achieved through the appropriate arrangement of the institutions of governance. One institution has been notably lacking from this institutional discussion – the institution of public bureaucracy.

"We are robots, aren't we?"

Bureaucracy is a central part of modern governance. Bureaucracy's practice and the systems it operates represent, in the mechanical terms beloved of

19th-century commentators, the engine of the physical and socio-economic reproduction of the liberal democratic state. This present practice is based not in wider civic aims as Woodrow Wilson and Waldo had hoped, but in a 'neutrality' that is inextricably tied to the needs and narratives of the market economy and to economic efficiency as the test for what is right. Its internal practice leaves it just as inflexible, distant, siloed and controlling as Weber posited, but it now works in a climate of increasing demands, resource constraints and managerialist performance expectations. This modern bureaucracy is as unreflective and risk-averse as its forebears. Its entire armoury is designed to direct others through the exercise of technocratic and financial control and with a focus on achieving generalized material benefits while allowing restricted societal input.

The present purpose of bureaucratic governance is unexpressed but is revealed in its practice. This is the economic efficiency of the state, measured in bureaucratic tests of value for money, cost–benefit, impact on business, growth and jobs. All programmes need to justify their impact on these concerns regardless of their purpose. The measure of public service delivery is cost-effectiveness with little focus on testing effectiveness towards what goals. Beyond issues as to the acceptability of public services to citizens or, increasingly, 'customers', there is no interest in how public administration might foster a sense of civic values or virtue. People are viewed as rational economic actors who must appreciate decisions taken in the interest of the general economy. It is a system which is unable to understand and address the fundamental challenges before it because they pose a threat to its unstated rational underpinnings. As one practitioner confided at interview: "We are robots, aren't we?"

The absence of a stated rationale leaves bureaucracy without a clear legal or constitutional frame for its activities. The combination of tools with a narrow economic focus, the production of policy and regulatory statements and systems which make assumptions about the public good, and the attempts at personal sense-making by individual public servants has no overt guiding rationale. Instead, this is seen as purely a matter for the government of the day to shape during its terms of office and for bureaucrats to trim the system they operate to catch its breeze. This would not be grave if the unstated rationale addressed the understandings of the 21st century, but it does not. It continues to assume that the complex interlinked social and ecological systems revealed in the notion of sustainable development can be centrally managed in isolation, and that there will be market adjustments or technical fixes that can address the fundamental imbalances. So far this does not appear to be the case and time is running out.

Examination of innovations which have sought to address the concept of governing *for* sustainable development offer insights into the elements of a different form and purpose of bureaucracy and the issues they would need to address.

Performance and decision metrics matter

Competitive and incentive-based structures have permeated all aspects of society, from educational exam performance targets to workplace incentive schemes. The approach excludes as illegitimate other approaches which cannot be measured in the same examined way. Critique or funding flows from the success in playing the narrow accountability game rather than whether any good is done. The overall result of this form of accountability has been to shift focus from the original civic republican aims of propriety and civics to a managerial focus on regulatory compliance and control. The focus of governance in recent years has been on specific performance targets for programmes or activities, alongside increased use of project management disciplines originally designed for ICT programmes. Governments and businesses are increasingly held to account against these managerialist targets and forecasts. Such targets are essentially distorting in systemic terms since no target can capture fully the nature of a desired change. Making the target the focus of work means that it becomes the end in itself rather than the original wider purpose. It prompts gaming of the governance system.

Much of this approach assumes people are naturally shirkers who have to be coerced to act. Civic republicanism by contrast expects people to be good actors and provides incentives of approbation and positive narratives, leaving the controls for bad actors as a firm backstop. This tallies with research that has identified the positive motivation of service for public administrators (Harney, 2002).

The machine of bureaucracy reaches for ready ideas and words from fashionable trends – ecological modernization, New Public Management – that draw on narratives that chiefly reinforce and sustain the focus on economic efficiency. The tendency to mimic analogue organizations or adopt existing norms is powerful and creates convergence in thinking and approaches institutionally. Mimetics is also the way in which new fashions and trends are reproduced across sectors or disciplines. The adoption of practices in Foucault's terms establishes or reinforces regimes of truth. The modernist and managerialist expectation of pace in governance pulls against the need for an inclusive contestability of governmental changes.

Considering Foucault's framing of governmentality, the current approach to accountabilities creates a disciplinary framework which incentivizes delivery of specific elements of public service action, limits local territorial variation or self-determination in favour of centralized prioritization and increases hierarchical management. It reinforces order, oversight and sectoral division. By reframing this against a civic and ecological perspective, setting minimization of domination at its heart, we can see the way towards a new milieu.

The elements of a new civic bureaucracy

Figure 5.1 reimagines governmentality that is driven by new civic and ecological goals and how its instruments would change. Only institutions and procedures survive from Figure 1.1 in this book, but these institutions and processes would need to be very different to support the new governmentality.

Foucault described the output of governmentality as the production of statements – a very appropriate term for bureaucratic endeavour. Most of my bureaucratic career, when I was not in project or management meetings or appearing before committees, was spent writing public policy papers and statutory guidance, submitting written reports or advice, or drafting letters.

Montesquieu's 'empire of laws' means that such statements and Weber's files will still be an important part of the bureaucratic function, but the civic republican ethic demands a more outgoing, engaging role for bureaucracy. The challenge of governing for the 21st century requires reflexive institutions which are able to learn and connect and embrace richness over reductionism.

The 21st-century challenges of limits to growth, the rise of right populism and the crisis of democratic governance require a move away from the industrial modernist model of economic efficiency and controlling government based in knowledge-power and uniformity. They need a governance which can build societal dialogue, reaffirming individual participation in decisions, empowering communities by acknowledging they have a say in shaping where they live, and building just bridges between

Figure 5.1: Civic and ecological governmentality

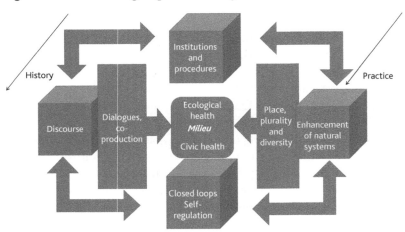

past, present and future and between differing groups in society. A public bureaucracy on this model would be released from the distant, controlled and controlling bureaucracy with its narrow rules, accountabilities and centralized expert decision-making. In its stead would come an enabling bureaucracy supporting socially just co-production with civil society and fostering place-based governance and collaborative, reflexive, systemic action.

As Weber and Foucault (and the political philosophers of the 'social contract' before them) recognize, the exercise of power requires an acceptance of the narratives of its legitimacy. Heath (Heath, 2020) has suggested this might be found in better pursuit of the optimization of equality, liberty and efficiency as the liberal tests of the common good. Better application of economic Pareto optimization could then drive fresh bureaucratic endeavour. Denhardt and Denhardt, with their focus on services, see dialogue and co-production as the keys to legitimacy. My own view is that these are each insufficiently radical. Amending the existing efficiency tools of bureaucracy as Heath suggests may allow elements of other considerations to be technocratically considered but they do nothing for democratization of control or repurposing of governance. They still assume there is a correct efficient central answer. Dialogue and co-production are vital, but without the underpinning of empowering institutional structures and legal protections for the plurality of voices and for nature and future generations, the necessary redistribution of power and the reconnections of the environmental and the social are unlikely to take root. The new neutrality of civic bureaucracy needs to be found not in a continuing economic rationality or a widening of participation but in a new role of helping to support the wider polity and to reconnect society with itself, its place and the environment in which it is situated.

This is, in essence, a bureaucracy whose narratives and practice place sustainable development and civic dialogue as its *raison d'être*, in place of bureaucracy's current practice of narrow economic efficiency and technocratic control. Given the depth to which current practice is imbued with a very different ethos, this change will require not simply new purpose and values as set out in the Welsh Government's Well-being Act and the *buen vivir* constitution. As we have seen in the many examples of the constraining impact of existing narratives and practice, transformative approaches will require comprehensive change in the detailed practice – the tools and technologies – of bureaucracy.

In place of the controlling *biopouvoir* that seeks to order society towards economic ends, a civic bureaucracy would use tools of inclusion and dialogue. They would value and foster diversity and local distinctiveness over uniformity and predictability. They would be supportive of creative and emergent delivery rather than specifying means as well as ends. They would allow connections to be made between the interacting social and ecological systems and seek to work to enable society to optimize outcomes rather than continuing to have goals compete within their own divided structures. Their new toolkit would test for domination, making explicit the winners and losers in decision-making, and would look beyond the human to the impacts of activity on the natural environment and planetary health. Regulation, funding and processes would focus on protecting and enhancing natural systems and improving civic engagement and inclusion. They would not be used to support the market or economy, which would instead function within, and have voice in delivering, the ecological and civic framework. As required in civic republican theory, a civic bureaucracy would not be controlling but enable conditions for different discussions and ultimately decisions to be made. This takes Foucault and Pettit's challenge of applying a focus on non-domination, dispersal of power and contestability to the detailed practice of bureaucracy.

Taking the examples of emerging practice and legislation on governance for sustainability worldwide, informed by Foucault's arguments on the impacts of domination and 'knowledge-power', the new civic bureaucracy would use sustainable development as a guiding ethic. This ethic would enrich the existing concepts of New Public Service and of New Public Governance, shaping public bureaucracy's role as a co-producing partner in design and delivery rather than a solo decision-taker and commissioner of action and infrastructure. The new public bureaucracy would use its expertise humbly to inform and support action that linked environment, society and economy rather than aiming to control individual aspects. It would seek out, respect and apply different forms of knowledge and it would foster locally determined action.

Such a change in practice and norms will be a substantial programme of work but it can draw on a wealth of discourses that offer the basis for new institutions and toolkits:

- Challenges to traditional economic method from the broad field of heterodox economics, including an interest in 'foundational economics' and 'livelihoods' over a focus on growth, non-growth economics and critique of competition and rational choice theory.
- Arguments from a range of disciplines to embrace systems thinking and complexity, most notably implications of General Systems Theory (Skyttner, 2005) for framing issues.
- Sustainability science with its focus on connectedness, participation and interaction of socio-economic systems.
- Post-modern organizational development theory that considers the idea of 'organization becoming', rather than control and direction, and advocates enabling leadership.
- Co-design and co-production values and techniques that allow people and communities to define their needs and opportunities rather than 'have good done to them'.

- Recognition of the role and legitimacy of indigenous and local forms of knowledge, alongside technical expertise, emerging from international development practice.
- Challenges to the siloed structuring of educational systems and disciplines, including from theories of experiential learning.
- Interest in reflexivity and uncertainty in governance in response to complexity in place of the planning and control model.
- Critique of competitive majoritarian representative democracy as the means to ensure inclusive societal benefits.

New civic bureaucracy: making it real

At a time of often increasing lionization of dominance over others: xenophobic right nationalism, partisanship, a polarizing social media, conspiracy theories and cynicism about public life, considering an ethos for bureaucracy of non-domination and civic participation in the context of the challenge of sustainable development can look daunting or, worse, naïve. Yet the values and practice explored in this book can offer a very real alternative to existing governance norms dominated by classical economic theory and tools. These alternatives are well founded in considerations of the social functioning of society and of how governance can be structured to promote civic concern and inclusivity over faction and exclusion. This is a governance based not on fostering competition between individuals in the name of efficiency and maximizing financial return but instead on building bridges and understandings in the name of civic and planetary health.

Such changes will require both political and societal will and a serious eye for detail – detail especially about processes and language. It will also need opportunity. Wales was able to make progress at the juncture where it became partially self-governing for the first time in 600 years and while its form of governance was still in flux and resistant to a competitive model. Similar points of departure can exist in governance of established states where one change can be a platform for reflexion and action.

At the close of *Republicanism: A Theory of Freedom and Government*, Pettit summarizes the characteristics he identifies as important to non-domination in relation to the organization of the state. These include:

- the empire-of-law condition, according to which government should operate by general law, not case by case;
- the dispersion-of-power constraint, according to which governmental power should be divided out among many hands;
- the counter-majoritarian condition, according to which it should be made more rather than less difficult for majority will to change at least certain fundamental areas of law;

- the recognition of the inevitability of the need for discretion in the exercise of governmental roles;
- the contestatory condition, to guarantee that the exercise of discretion is not hostile to the interests and ideas of people at large, or of some section of the community.

Applying this to the role of bureaucracy, a civic republican approach would recognize positively some elements of bureaucratic practice. It would see elements of balance of powers in the structures and checks and balances. It would endorse the concern about propriety and avoidance of corruption in public administration. It would also be interested by the potential of a non-political public service rather than interest politics. The civic republican in the mould of James Madison would, however, be deeply troubled by the controlling nature of public administration, the desire for uniformity, its siloed nature, its narrow economic focus and practice and its failure to reflect and encourage diversity, place and community. They would be concerned by the technocratic distance from the impacts on citizens. They would find its linkage to majoritarian democracy unsettling. They would find the system as a whole disempowering of local action, civic engagement or public understanding. They would find the rush to simple answers and responses a poor substitute for consideration and debate.

Before considering this new bureaucracy, it is important to remember that changes need to apply across the whole of bureaucratic endeavour. A focus purely on the policy or planning or service roles of bureaucracy will only scratch the surface of its impact. Well-constructed policy, law or plans can founder on the normative assumptions of bureaucracy as to how things should be delivered. Every public administrator shapes a relationship with civil society – be it in the tone of a letter, an approach to an interview or through the design of standard forms and notices. Change, therefore, needs to go across the board. It should be reflected in how finance, grant management, audit, regulation, project management, service delivery, correspondence and human resources operate as much as in policy work. Change will need to address in full 'the stable, recurring, repetitive, patterned nature of the behaviour that occurs within institutions, and because of them' (Goodin, 1996, 22).

Changing the practice and purpose of bureaucracy will not in itself change the self-reproduction of the existing system of governance but it will provide opportunity to challenge inherited norms and their metrics and narratives. As Voß and Bornemann close their article on governance designs for sustainable development: 'Politics cannot be escaped or bypassed, nor eliminated or completely controlled by governance designs, but they can be analyzed and reflected on in order to devise more robust design strategies for new reflexive forms of governance' (Voß and Bornemann, 2011). *Pace* Voß and Bornemann, the civic bureaucratic function must not bypass nor control politics – that is, in Marx's words, for it to become civil society itself. As a career bureaucrat I have always deeply respected those who put themselves forward for the public vote and give so much of their time in pursuit of public service. To draw on Wilson's analogy, they are the fires that drive our existing engine of government. But bureaucracy should become an active and creative aid to civic debate and work to level the playing field of democracy, reshaping or replacing its toolkit accordingly.

Following through the implications of new purpose will generate new toolkits. Some of these tools have been identified in the last chapter but not all the tools that may be needed currently exist. Legal changes that drive new actions and narratives will prompt them to be developed and tested.

The new civic bureaucracy will need formal assessments which show those who specifically benefit or suffer disbenefit from schemes in full rather than in abstract or in aggregated numbers. It will need new forms and techniques of engagement which empower and connect communities. It will need to reterritorialize thinking and decisions. It will need to reconsider the existing systems of control from land use to market regulation to see how they can better support the aim of civic reconnection and enable a plurality rather than a uniformity of ways of living. It will help to apply the same tests to international co-operation among democratic states and how that can support the same goals internationally. Above all, perhaps, it will help to reconnect society to the environment as our ultimate life support system not as a dumping ground or an infinite source of easy profit.

This role for public administration in this model is both steering *and* serving. Steering, in the sense of operating a fresh framework of processes and rules which minimize domination, and serving, because such a framework would be focused on supporting inclusion and engagement for all. In other words, serving would be set within a legal governance framework, one based in Brundtland's sense of needs, not as simply as a response to market demands. This would be a bureaucracy which supported the effective work of the polity, in an echo of the accidental unitary governance Wales enjoyed in the early years of devolution before old assumptions of the 'right' way to govern reasserted themselves.

The following sections set out pen portraits of the rationale for changes and sources and ideas for new practice, alongside potential changes in legal provisions to support them. A headline summary of the old and new forms of practice, organization, and purpose and function for bureaucracy is set out for reference in Tables 5.3–5.5.

The centrality of deliberation and discourse

As we have seen, the idea of civic dialogue and participation was hard-wired into thinking on governance for sustainable development in the introduction to the Brundtland Report. It features heavily in the responses of sustainable development practitioners. The corresponding academic literature of governing for sustainable development and some of the more innovative governance practice, draws on a civic republican notion of the importance of civic dialogue to foster new mutual understandings and build reflexive transformations. This is best exemplified by the work of John Dryzek (Dryzek, 2005) who has wrestled with the form of dialogue that can support such transformation. He has termed the form of civic dialogue and civil society activism that he believes to be best suited 'discursive' rather than deliberative democracy in order to distinguish it from the more formal settings to which deliberative democracy has often been applied.

Philip Pettit sets out clearly in his (post-)modern exposition of civic republicanism exactly why such dialogue is viewed as important. For civic republicanism it has two benefits:

- It helps to promote civic virtue by placing people in a civic space where they have to at least be seen to consider the needs of others rather than pursue naked self-interest.
- It extends the degree of appreciation of a plurality of beliefs and views by causing people to have to see the world through the eyes of others.

The first point echoes Jürgen Habermas' writing on ideal speech and communicative rationality. This is based in thinking on the role of language in discourse or dialectic (communicative action) as building rational reflection on the 'life world' which constitutes individual understanding (Habermas, 1987). The great writer on totalitarianism, Hannah Arendt, argued that civic dialogue created an enlarged mentality that could appreciate value pluralism. She posited that the individual needs the presence of (different) others to be prompted to think critically and to self-question. She extended this in her writing on the Eichmann trial to see the root of evil as being primarily an unthinkingness, a lack of self-reflection, often demonstrated in the parroting of banal dogma (Arendt, 2003).

For those who prefer an economic rationale for dialogue, Elinor Ostrom, in her Nobel Prize winning economic work on governance of the Commons (Ostrom, 2009), demonstrated empirically how dialogue and shared rules across landscape management can deliver legitimate and sustained localized governance. Related economic work in games theory has shown how prior dialogue between individual actors can positively shape the outcome of the response to game dilemmas. Ostrom is also an originator of the concept of co-production of public services (Ostrom and Ostrom, 1977) which has become increasingly important within recent thinking on public service and has extended from its origins in shaping client relationships to wider co-working on public policy and delivery (Alford, 2014).

A major concern in writing on dialogue is the relationship between civil society and government. Habermas in his early writings believes that government is a negative influence that fills the public space and prevents a perfect speech situation. Like Liberals, Marxists, Weberians and civic republicans, Habermas worries that bureaucracy is by its nature too controlling and prone to take away the independent life of civil society, or, as he prefers, the 'public sphere'. Others see the necessity for government to engage as partners to enable civic dialogue while guarding against the risk of administrative control and allowing space and freedom for a variety of formative agents (Dryzek and Pickering, 2019, 129). A second academic and practical concern about dialogue is that it can be dominated by powerful interests. This is a major governance concern of civic republicanism and is ultimately why civic republicanism sees an important role for legally based government and public administration to hold the ring against such interests. A third concern, seen mostly in green political writing, is that dialogue might deliver the 'wrong' answers. This could be because it operates within the existing context for decisions which lack a relationship to nature and provide no direct voice for nature or future generations in processes of dialogue. The first is reflected in a stance of radical ecologism which seeks a transformatory shift in civic understanding and action (Dobson, 2007) while the latter has prompted ideas such as mandating representative proxies for nature (Eckersley, 2004) including law and activism in the field of rights for nature.

Foucault further cautions us (Fornet-Betancourt et al, 1987, 298), with a dig at Habermas, that there can be no 'utopia of perfectly transparent communication' as all speech acts are games of power, seeking in some sense to influence another person. The art is to ensure that these are conducted with the minimal intent to dominate. Contestability of process can be an important aid to this.

While the literature on dialogue is extensive and persuasive, it generally falls short of offering clear process for bureaucratic arrangements. The focus to date has been on formal forms of advisory and decision processes such as public arbitration, public hearings and citizen juries, and on measures promoting transparency and public access to information.

Co-production/co-design

Much of my recent interest in governance has been focused on exploring the practical application of co-production and co-design at place and landscape scales. The essence of co-production and co-design is to work with those impacted by decisions or issues to design and implement solutions that they have shaped rather than a technocratic or patriarchal 'doing good to people'. Co-production serves to reduce the social distancing inherent in technocracy.

The approach has been applied in work to change the patient–doctor relationship to one where the patient manages their condition with advice from the medical practitioners rather than being a passive recipient. The approach has also been used increasingly in international development work to redress the balance of power between funders and recipients and build on local knowledge rather than import solutions. More generally it has been taken up in social interventions including regeneration programmes and youth justice. Recently co-production principles have been applied to areas of public policy development and decision-making that were previously the reserve of consultation processes.

For co-production to work, there has to be a genuine shift in power. That shift should typically be bounded by wider rules or principles agreed by participants but these need to be carefully designed to avoid the shift of power moving to the point where it is not credible to participants or where it allows traditional sources of power to overrule. Those supporting co-production need to be careful about their exercise of expertise and be open to, and encourage, different ways of looking at a situation rather than promoting or sustaining traditional assumptions about what interventions to make and what constitutes a positive outcome. This openness to 'indigenous knowledge' improves the information available for all participants in debate and decisions.

Co-production also needs to ensure a breadth of participation. If it fails to capture the range of views across a community or institutional or subject setting, or notably favours the role of some participants over others, it will reinforce existing power structures and assumptions rather than making new connections and building wider understanding.

Co-production needs detailed design and appropriate facilitation (Quinn and de Vrieze, 2019, and Appendix 2). One aim of co-production is to enable the sharing of the range of worldviews (Koltko-Rivera, 2004) of participants and to understand others' perspectives on issues and learn from them. Table 5.1 shows a product of a co-produced dialogue undertaken with members of a landscape scale partnership in rural Wales. Here, the participants received collective feedback on the expressions they had used in sectoral focus groups to describe their relationship to nature. This work provided one basis for them to consider their respective starting approaches to discussion.

Depending on the circumstances, work in co-production may draw on experience from conflict transformation in exploring underlying factors and views (Francis, 2002). Co-production often applies arts practice to provide formats that engage a wide section of participants, tap into non-rational values and free them from the competitive focus of existing dialogue process (Pearson et al 2018).

As a supplement to the 2018 work, I and my colleague Willow Leonard-Clarke undertook a series of walking interviews with farmers

Table 5.1: Relationships to nature

Group/typology	Master	Steward	Partner	Participant
Farmer	Create landscapes			
Grazier		Care, stewardship		
Landowner	Custodian			
Forester	Create woodland			
Nature Trust			Reveal stewardship	Voice for nature
Heritage Trust		Maintenance, protection		
Water company	Custodian			
Regulator	Management	Protection	Restoration	

Source: Quinn (2018).

in a catchment partnership in the Brecon Beacons National Park. The farmers appreciated the time for them to talk about their land and their relationship to it. During the course of the walk on each of their land holdings, each moved from the language of the commercial business standpoint expected of them by the bureaucratic system to expressing their feelings about nature, the generations who had gone before them, their pride and excitement in the work, and their aspirations for the future. This richer and more emotive narrative provides a basis for different ways of considering the nature of farming and for making connections with others (Table 5.2).

Legal scope

In civic republican theory, fostering civic dialogue should be a feature of all functions of public bureaucracy. To avoid arbitrary or coercive processes, such civic dialogue should be legally framed (remembering the injunction of 'empire of laws not men') for each significant process of interaction, as well as being a guiding principle of public life. This would need to be expressed as new (often, replacement) process duties and rights specific to different circumstances. The less formal forms of participation are as important as set piece institutional events such as citizens' juries or inquiries for the day-to-day policy work and less intimidating.

Given the potential perverse impacts of precisely specifying forms of engagement, the legal scope should not specify exact processes but define the intent of co-production and allow for accompanying working guidance which can be formally adopted by institutions and contested or called upon by civil society.

Towards a New Civic Bureaucracy

Table 5.2: Farmer expressions of utility and feeling

Utility	Feeling
Investment	*Opportunity; ambition; confidence; risk; challenge; choice; answers; learning*
Suitable, appropriate	*Do what's right, it would be wrong; it's all about context; taken out of context; narratives on place and natural surroundings*
Enhance, improve, maximize	*Proud; personal satisfaction; lucky; fortunate; make a difference; that'd be nice; that's nice to see; passion; vision; happy*
Location; tourism	*Place; our space; lovely place; beautiful; pleasant; it doesn't get much better; spectacular view; cracking view; amazing; belonging; feel part of it; community; trust uniqueness; special; strength; pride; family; legacy; integrity; opportunity; responsibility; need to take care of it; lucky; privileged; enjoyment; luxury; do it right; happy; my favourite place; hope; pleasure; atmosphere; love; peaceful; protection; narratives on place and natural surroundings*
Manage	*You go with it, create, shape, control; custodian; responsibility; care; got to look after it; duty*
Productive	*Challenge; hardworking; proud; happy; personal satisfaction; enjoy*
Marketing	*Anti-farmer; farmer bashing; worry; frustration; concern; a story; misinformed*
Unproductive land	*Chance; ambition; excitement; concern*
Evidence base; modelled information; measurement; quantify	*Experience; I know; narratives on place and natural surroundings*
Improved infrastructure	*Tidy; do a tidy job; a picture of a farm; pride; do a good job; care; satisfaction; the way it should be; happy*
Market a product	*Good quality; history; family; place; stories; upset; nasty; frustration*
Partnerships	*Challenge; conflict; different views; shared vision; misunderstanding; trust; honest; open; learning; interesting*

For delivery organizations, a guiding principle of dialogue would be to serve to humanize and personalize the experience – a phone call rather than a formal letter, a site meeting rather than a formal notice. Processes would strive to build mutual understanding and learning and the potential for more reflexive actions. Frontline staff would have greater discretion as to how best to deliver broad goals rather than following precise protocols. In place of the impenetrable legal form letter and the buried sentence about rights to challenge in writing, there would be clarity as to the process and the opportunity to discuss. This would mean providing more human capacity rather the focus on online service and 'bots'.

In regulatory roles, dialogue processes strengthen the quality and mutual understanding of decisions. They help to avoid technocratic or sectoral capture and can foster dialogue between polluters and residents, bringing out important issues or knowledges of communities affected by decisions. There would be legal requirements for formal co-production of proposals with affected communities (including businesses) rather than brief dissemination of developed proposals and consultation.

In policy development, government's convening role is central to establishing broad dialogue. The bilateral, sectoral relationships of competitive, representative systems breed clientelism, capture and single voices over dialogue. By bringing different considerations of an issue together, in contrast to the separation of inputs required in formal consultation, business, government and communities face mutual critique and the potential for mutual learning. Business should be present rather than the present approach in which business interests are often treated separately in government and benefit from separate impact testing provision in law and regulatory processes. Including business within civic society debate serves to link them with the impact of their decisions. It also helps to address the barrier of the fear of market reaction in states seeking to take steps towards sustainable development. Business itself has begun to adopt public value as an aspect of its work. Public value is now central to some business schools, including that at my own Cardiff University. B Corp members commit to contributing to society and the World Business Council for Sustainable Development is a voice in support of serious action on global environmental concerns.

Policy and programme development should have a legal menu of co-production or dialogue options, the application of which to a particular case can be challenged by civil society. Standing processes of dialogue or co-production, for example working groups shaping long-term change, should have a formal legal status and time-frames, whose application would again be challengeable without recourse to the courts by civil society. The results of those processes should carry great legal weight in decision-making to avoid the risk of arbitrary dismissal or abandonment. As a counterbalance to potential bureaucratic control of the agenda, there should be an open ability to call for or establish legal deliberative fora to address issues, thus giving scope for initiation from sectors other than government.

Reterritorialization: the importance of place

Civic republicanism views place-based governance as an important check on centralizing power and a champion of diversity and plural values as well as a forum for dialogue and decision. Place, however, is problematic for the existing practice of bureaucracy. Place challenges the norms of uniformity, separation of functions and distanced, dispassionate decision-making. Place-based working will typically cut across bureaucratic and expert divisions, being messy, interlinked, emotional and complex. In the Weberian conception of bureaucracy, place will always be in tension with the fulfilment of the specific expert and rule-based function – be that function the building of a road or the pursuit of policy on housing – and any attempt to seek to reflect more roundly the needs of place may be seen as subjective and hence suspect.

Governance for sustainable development sees place as key to transformatory governance of coupled socio-economic systems (Horlings et al, 2020) because of the very challenges and opportunities it presents. Place has distinctive features for transformatory governance:

- Place is a forum of shared social experience, of dialogue and potential communal governance.
- Place is a means of redressing the modernist tradition of separation and distancing by reconnecting actors with the consequences, social or environmental, of decisions.
- Place is a means of recognizing and being reflexive towards interlocking social-ecological systems.

Place is immediately relevant to those who live and/or work there. Working at a place level can connect people to wider decision-making and political concerns that otherwise feel abstract and distant. Place is also inherently connected. It is formed and understood from the interaction of its elements not the separation of them. It therefore provides a counterweight to the separation and specialization inherent in governance structures. Simone Weil describes this with rhetorical flourish in her striking work, *L'enracinement* ('The need for roots') (Weil, 2002, 68), written in exile to guide a post-war France, when she says: 'When connections are cut, each thing is looked at as an end in itself. Uprootedness breeds idolatry.' For these same reasons, a focus on place offers a subversion of existing norms and presents an opportunity for new forms of bureaucratic practice that view place as a starting point rather than an inconvenience. Place-based working offers new technologies of power that shift the balance to the local and the systemic rather than the centralizing and the technocratic. Place offers a more rooted and rich sense for considering resilience and reflexivity in governance. Instead of the macro abstraction of economic theory, place offers a focus on the detailed structures, capacities and opportunities. Place is also a medium for interaction that can at its best cut across hierarchy and social and political divides and connect people as people. In this way it can provide a basis for increasing equality and reducing the scope for 'othering' of disadvantage or different status.

A new civic bureaucracy

The formal legal process of management of land is one of Foucault's core elements of the technology of governmentality. It is deeply rooted in its reflection of the existing views of managerialist control, economic efficiency, property rights and technocracy. The institutions of land use planning focus primarily on realizing modernist economic goals and operate in the face of local communities to technocratic mechanisms, despite the well-established calls for societally-engaged 'collaborative planning' (Healey, 2005). Both planning and urban regeneration have typically been done 'to' communities that occupy problematized places rather than done 'with' them. Many of the improvements or 'treatments' have had the effect of moving on the people rather than changing their lot, as characterized by gentrification of areas in the urban context. The functions and systems of land use planning are likely to require a systemic change not simply a rebadging of purpose. The concept of sustainable place-making provides a good starting point for reform, provided it is carried through the whole of the values system of territorial development.

Dialogue in places can concretize and connect views. Figure 5.2 shows the forms of language used by participants in a major landscape scale partnership in Wales when asked to describe their place. Shared sense of place can be a factor in enabling transformatory socio-ecological change (Grenni et al, 2020). As Ostrom's work demonstrated (Ostrom, 2009), shared physical space such as common land or community landscapes also provides opportunities for collaborative and collective management in place of state-controlled governance instruments.

The most noted example of landscape-scale collaboration in governance is the New York City water catchment. This involves a partnership between the water company, local farmers and the local communities to manage the water quality in the upper New York State catchment at source as an

Figure 5.2: Language of partners about the Brecon Beacons

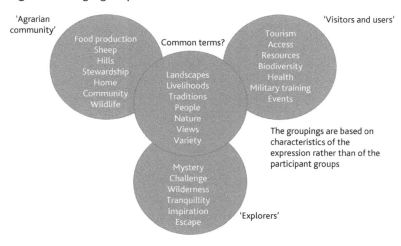

alternative to making major end-of-pipe investment in cleaning technologies (Hoffman, 2010). The approach relies on a collective management structure, real-time remote monitoring and self-regulation.

Place is central to practices of community-led planning. The practice of asset-based regeneration challenges existing regeneration practice of seeing places as asset-less and valueless and hence due for replacement (Hart, 1997). The 'deep place' perspective on sustainable place-making has suggested a perspective based on different understandings of growth and economy, in which the social, environmental and cultural sustainability of places and communities is enhanced (Lang and Marsden, 2018). Challenges to the hegemony of the land use planning system have been more limited. Self-build housing schemes have operated in a niche of local authority provided sites in the UK, while community-led housing development still faces significant hurdles (Heywood, 2016). The broad community development movement has also faced barriers in its aim of empowering communities (Eversole, 2012). Existing forms of community-based participative planning has attracted criticism of risking coercion rather than engaging (Alwaer and Cooper, 2019). Alternative low impact communities have also struggled to achieve recognition within the aims of the existing system, as demonstrated by the complexity faced by the One Planet Living movement in the UK.

Legal scope

Institutional design would embed responsibilities at different scales, using the principle of subsidiarity to ensure issues are always dealt with as locally as is possible. This is best reflected in formal and clear legal divisions of responsibility. Ideally this separation is backed by a constitution in order to restrict the scope of any interventions between tiers. Bodies at different levels would be mandated to work with communities in places to connect between the impacts of differing functional responsibilities.

Public bodies would be required to organize to have local presence and delivery structures that combine their range of functional responsibilities. These could be physically delivered alongside other bodies or local public entities. There would be a requirement for these local entities to contribute locally to sustainability and civic responsibility. This would be undertaken against the definition in national law or constitution and as identified in local assessments, and this work should be communicated publicly. Where possible public functions and controls would be delivered through community-led organizations rather than governmental structures.

In the spirit of non-domination and sustainable development, central land use planning would be replaced by localized sustainable place-making subject to protections and enhancements for natural systems. This would be based in community and place-based processes of decision-making and be stripped of the predict and provide responsibilities for delivery of outcomes presently mandated by the state. The scope of this discursive sustainable place-making would be determined by the locality and not be concerned by issues of uniformity or control for economic efficiency. It would be informed by public information on natural systems, local assets and well-being. The process would be co-produced and open to civic challenge. Larger than local developments would need legal sign-off from all local communities affected. Higher tiers would only test proposals for new infrastructure against pursuit of civic and ecological health rather than as support to general economic growth.

New ways of knowing

As we have seen, the bureaucratic tradition has a very particular, often unstated, way of knowing. The way of knowing derives from rational empirical and economic ways of viewing what counts and uses bounded and numerical metrics for measuring value. The present approach values measurable numbers over other forms of knowledge and applies a proxy Pareto optimization and statistical and economic methods to reduce a plurality of impacts and values to a data point. The approach is strongly biased towards financial and economic data – part of the 'pathological path dependency' of states and administration to foreground the economic (Dryzek and Pickering, 2019). Conventional appraisal techniques have put considerable weight on estimates of monetizable benefits and costs. This tends to give a false sense of certainty around decisions and can lead to putting little weight on impacts that cannot be turned into cash numbers. At their worst they can fail to reflect the purpose of the policy. Applying discount rates to cost–benefit assessments favours near-term spending over investment in long-term action and benefits.

The continued underpinning of Weberian bureaucratic structure protects the bureaucrat from thinking about the wider implications or impacts of a decision. The things which need to be considered are largely predetermined and limited. They follow a *zweckrationalität* of the function assigned to the bureaucrat and the tools made available to deliver it. Much of the present approach has been captured in the notion of evidence-based policy making in which the concept of the policy cycle means that science informs, policy disposes and evaluation checks. Apart from being an ideal form that is extremely far from the lived experience of the bureaucrat, it is a technocratic circle which is primarily designed to justify a decision. It is disinterested in richness and distribution of impacts, relying on averages and reductionism. It places little weight on local knowledge, making connections between concerns, or sentiment. Although it intends to be neutral and to separate facts and values, it is inherently tied to the perceptions of truth and belief of the applied toolkit.

What is required for the new civic bureaucracy is not a dismissal of rationality but an *unbounding* of rationality and an *unlearning* of technocratic practice. This means the ability to accept and learn from different forms of knowledge and different forms of data and to share and discuss these different forms of knowledge with civil society (Fischer, 2003). It means the willingness to see and work with connections both spatially and cross-sectorally. It means a willingness to accept uncertainty and to proceed reflexively and relinquish the impression of control. It means to be radical in the use of social science, heeding C. Wright Mills' injunction in *The Sociological Imagination* (Mills, 1959) rather than applying it as a means of social control. Application of non-positivistic social science techniques, such as methods of naturalistic inquiry, would provide a broad basis for non-numerical information in decision-making and problem identification (Lincoln and Guba, 1985). Such approaches are very occasionally used in evaluations but never in my experience in policy development.

Option appraisal against objectives and non-numerical multi-criteria analysis of projects are designed to provide decision-makers and the public with raw information about the potential impact on different parameters. These are already available in programme and project management but can be overwhelmed by the application of the presently required cost–benefit analysis and net present value calculations. Appraisals also rarely take a participative approach to inputting to the qualitative assessments, often relying on survey and decision support software.

Modelling, forecasting and scenarios have become increasingly part of the bureaucratic toolkit in response to complexity and uncertainty. These need to be approached with caution. In my experience they all tend towards seeking to offer certainty from the complexity. This feeds conventional decision-making rather than enriching dialogue. They are also very much subject to their assumptions which are very rarely presented transparently for a lay audience or made available for the input of different assumptions or starting data. Using Bayesian designs can at least provide probabilities for both the parameters and the hypotheses used in modelling. Very simple visual models, like systems maps, can be used as a prompt to dialogue.

Legal scope

Work should not prioritize specialist forms of knowledge over the understandings of local and affected people. The views of impacts and interconnections should be gathered and highlighted. Assessments would include impacts on the non-human.

The forms of analysis to be applied to appraisals and forecasts would be required to be compatible with the discursive goals of the new bureaucracy. Modelling, if used at all, would need to make its assumptions and boundaries transparent and be used to inform rather than drive decisions and debate. Models should be open to challenge. Rational choice theory should be used sparingly and be informed by understanding of the limitations of its application, in particular the extent to which in real situations, people choose irrationally and the extent to which their preferences change over time – important in long-term decisions.

Discounting to net present value would not generally be applied in order to offset the human tendency to value near-term benefit higher than long-term benefit (the idea on which the concept of discounting is founded).

All appraisals would assess the distribution of impacts in detail – the precise winners and losers – and not reduce this to a single composite output. Common, mandated questions might include examples such as: Who benefits and loses from change – very specifically – does this reduce inequalities? Does this benefit civic engagement? Does this increase ecological health? Who benefits from inaction? What risks do we face? What risks are we storing for the future? Does this impinge on any group or place?

Enabling action not controlling it

At present, there is very little bureaucratic practice in relation to the management of actions that is not controlling. Current governance uses competitive access to financing as a prime means of directing behaviour. These are not subject to the checks and balances of regulatory actions. This has potential to drive clientelism and reduces the scope for creativity and genuine public value. This is reinforced by the discipline of audit and the target-based performance management of public administrators and grant recipients which drives a narrow accountability, often predetermines inputs and outputs, and disables or reflexive or creative action. Controls assume most participants are bad actors and rather than supporting them in finding positive outcomes, it seeks to monitor and penalize them against performance indicators using a contractual model. The onus is placed on the applicant to navigate the complexities of the funding system, leading to inequalities of access.

An alternative enabling approach can build on notable elements of theory and practice, many of which have arisen in response to the limitations of New Public Management. New Public Governance (Osborne, 2020) and ideas of public value leadership place an alternative emphasis on collaborative public service and the importance of metagovernance – the governance of governance (Torfing and Triantafillou, 2013). In public value theory, all public service actions, including funding relationships, may be regarded as services and it is the service user, not the provider, who creates public value in the co-production of those services. Treating people as good actors and supporting rather than penalizing their efforts not only serves to give more resilient and reflexive outcomes but also increases social capital and civic engagement. The risk of deadweight in universal funding is an efficiency test which is less important for a civic perspective and means testing generally should be avoided. New Public Service (Denhardt and Denhardt, 2007) also points to the value of engaging citizens as a democratizing civic force under its mantra of 'serving not steering'. Redesigning the relationship with civil society can also draw on work on what makes for effective and lasting community partnerships (Getha-Taylor, 2019).

Legal scope

As civic republicanism is focused on the avoidance of self-interest and partisanship in public life, as well as the promotion of wider non-domination, there would be strict legal controls on:

- the basis for decision-making and funding;
- conflicts of interest;
- impropriety.

The focus on the importance of the rule of law would require decision-making, regulation and funding to be based in a transparent process which addressed a set of mandated tests. New funding and regulatory schemes would have to have a clear legal base and associated process. They would allow for contestation against their impact on civic and ecological health and there would be a presumption not to regulate or fund unless there was a clear positive contribution.

Law would require adequate time for process development and engagement. The emphasis should be on the minimum controls necessary for propriety rather making funding or regulation a series of hurdles for applicants. Application forms should be minimalist and focus on the details necessary to assure eligibility and propriety. Applicants should be supported through the process and have ready access to in-person support.

Funding and programmes would be based on clearly stated longer-term goals rather than requiring specific short-term milestones, targets or outputs. Applicants would be seen as delivery partners rather than contractors and be supported to receive funding and deliver outcomes reflexively.

Funding for individuals should be rights-based, easily obtained and generally universally provided as part of citizenship. Funding for projects or services should be openly available and need not be competitively awarded. Where there are a known number of potential providers, funding may be awarded in principle subject to agreement on terms. This changes the dynamic of traditional bidding or applications. Where there is not a known number of providers, focus should be on enabling new entrants to funding and testing the continuing contribution of existing recipients against clear criteria. Match funding should not be a general requirement for project funding so as not to disadvantage new entrants and less wealthy actors. Funding for public bodies or in general support of non-governmental organizations should normally only be hypothecated at a very high level of generality of purpose against the organization's remit to allow reflexivity within the legal framework.

Auditing and evaluation should be charged with a focus on the emergent qualities of work and seek to support improvement towards goals rather than punish non-compliance. They should be comfortable with uncertainty and look for reflexive responses. There would be a requirement for long-term reviews of programmes both against detailed purpose and its contribution to civic and ecological health.

Ways of organizing

The structures and processes of bureaucracy reproduce themselves in the civic sphere in the forms of sectoral divisions, competition and control. The classic and persistent form of bureaucratic organization combines hierarchical control, separation of function and specialization. It is interested in 'right-sizing' structures in the name of limiting the spread of command and for perceived economy of scale. Current structures create control centres which regulate and limit the work of others – Finance, Audit, Human Resources – rather than supporting teams and enabling dialogue.

Existing management mantras on institutional scales and hierarchical spread of controls intended to improve effectiveness have little basis in empirical study (Boyne, 2003), or, as Herbert A. Simon put it years earlier, we have 'proverbs' of administration rather than founded theories (Simon, 1946). There is an opportunity to rethink structures to work more connectedly and to have limited hierarchies and emphasis on heterarchies and networks, with greater responsibility given to the local levels. Regulating functions would be replaced with support functions. Technical expertise would be used to support issue formation and civic engagement.

Instead of modelling itself on a mechanical system for mechanical outcomes, bureaucracy instead needs to be organized and operate to mirror the civic and ecological values that it is seeking to support in society. It should be joined-up, thoughtful, human and respectful of difference. It needs to be itself reflexive in its operation and organization to meet the challenges of the present. This is in sharp contrast to practice drawn from the Weberian and

New Public Management conceptions of bureaucracy. The focus would be on serving the effectiveness of the polity.

Skills required for dialogue and co-production are noticeably different to those on which past recruitment has been focused. They include the ability to facilitate, learn, use knowledge lightly and humbly, and support rather than audit and control. Present systems of control limit the scope for effective co-production by retaining control and limiting frontline discretion (Brown and Head, 2019). New Public Governance and Public Value Leadership (Getha-Taylor et al, 2011) has suggested an alternative enabling role for bureaucratic leadership as a metagovernance role linking networks of actors within governance systems.

Legal scope

Legal requirements would be placed on the ability of the administrative design to address place, diversity and participation. The suggests a focus on multifunctional local teams with the backing of multifunctional technical support. The purpose of functions would be mandated against a framework of achieving good rather than simply preventing harm.

All functional units would be legally charged with the same civic purpose and goals and charged with collaboration to deliver defined civic benefit. Their contribution would be reported and open to public challenge. Functions would be required to internalize positive and negative impacts of their work and to focus with others on key change issues. Some functions are likely to need to be repurposed and some would be undertaken through community management and social rather than private provision.

Legislation would be codified to provide a clear linkage between activities and goals within a coherent, ideally constitutional setting. Precise process requirements would prevent arbitrary action and embed new ways of working. There would be adequate mandated funding for reform, with a particular focus on civic engagement.

There would be legal protection for public administrators from political or sectoral pressure in carrying out their legal functions. Political influence on appointments or promotions in the permanent administration would be circumscribed.

Internal performance systems and management structures would prioritize reflexivity, collective deliberation and civic engagement over control and authority.

New purpose and values

The economic purpose of governance and the efficiency purpose of bureaucracy are the major contextual barriers to the aim of governing for sustainable development and to addressing present civic governance challenges. Their unstated aims flow from this framing and are based in understanding of humankind as competitive and self-interested. The lauding of wealth and consumption over past decades underpins the present crisis in democratic governance and the collapse of planetary health. Public bureaucracy would need to be guided by new express legal goals if they are to operate in new ways.

Taking the models of Ecuador's or Bolivia's *buen vivir* constitution and Wales' Well-being Act indicates how a different expression of purpose could shift the frame and narrative of bureaucracy by replacing the unstated aims embedded in its stated neutrality. Establishing such express aims in law would need to be subject to widespread societal engagement. This discussion would be sharpened by being informed by the Brundtland ethic and the civic republican concept of non-domination to prevent it become a shopping list or committee drafting.

As in the Welsh case, definition of economic purpose is likely to be most contentious as it strikes at the heart of the present system and its assumptions. Civic bureaucracy would likely be more attuned to Main Street than Wall Street – it would consider the real economy of livelihoods and work. Heterodox economics provides a possible narrative language. It has a focus on social rather than individual action and different views from classical economics on supply and demand, surplus and the price signal, competition, rational choice and the impact of wages on production. It is interested in the local economy and in the distributive impacts of the operation of the economy as a whole. It considers that economic activity should flow from societal underpinnings not vice versa. Profitability not consumption/production is a guide to success.

Recent work in this field has focused on the concept of foundational economy (Foundational Economy Collective, 2018). This considers the role of activities that have to be delivered locally, many of which can most readily be met from the needs and abilities within the community itself, rather than the small proportion of the total economy that is traded and internationally mobile. This includes the role of the natural resources of the area – a fixed and continuing asset – and the extent to which these are being used sustainably to the benefit of the community or exploited and exhausted for external gain. It can therefore – unlike much conventional economic policy – have relevance for rural as well as urban areas. There is interest here too in the role of community ownership, commons and co-operatives as means of managing and distributing land, assets and incomes more communally.

In the context of limits to growth, work has also reconsidered the present economic growth model and suggested a steady state model, degrowth or a-growth based concepts of well-being and prosperity consonant with sustainable development and equity. The non-growth economy would be very different from the present one (Jackson, 2009) but the idea of a steady state economy has a long history, featuring in J.S. Mill's *Principles of Political Economy* (Mill, 1965).

Legal scope

There would be a set of legal purposive goals for public bureaucracy developed through a process of public dialogue. It would be informed by the concept of governing for sustainable development and of minimizing domination and would draw on the available international examples. The focus would be on broad civic benefits, inclusion, local voice and the governance of governance. Where legislative norms permit, there would be accompanying rights and duties.

Taking Montesquieu and the argument a step further: constitutionalism

The idea of a legal purpose and mandate for bureaucracy takes us into more overtly political waters. Views of public bureaucracy as its own potential force for civic good come up squarely against the charges of democratic illegitimacy posed by principal-agent views of bureaucracy in representative democracy and the long-standing fears of a powerful state bureaucracy.

As a senior bureaucrat, I often had an internal (and sometimes external) dialogue about whether I had legitimacy in pursuing a particular course or developing a process or idea. Yes, I had to have final political endorsement in some form, but that did not always feel enough. For all the politics that might surround it, a process towards establishing a legal purpose and role for bureaucracy – an empire of laws not men – has attractions. It would above all lay bare and test the assumptions underpinning public bureaucracy in liberal democratic states.

There are already existing legal provisions or guidance that legitimate some independent role for public administrators, but these are currently proscribed. There is not, in general, an actionable provision of duty to public service, though there may be a general link to upholding the constitution or the law. I have yet to find a circumstance where the constitutional separation of powers advocated by Montesquieu expressly covers the bureaucracy separate from the political executive, though I look forward to being corrected. While there was much discussion of (and extension to) the role of the US presidency in assuring the accountability of the executive during the Constitutional Convention, there was no separate provision made in the Constitution for the public administration itself. Indeed, they could not have conceived a public administration in the modern form.

The US Constitutionalist school of public administration nevertheless considers that the Constitution can and does provide a reference basis for the operation of the public administration (Newbold, 2010). The school reflects on three aspects: the civic republican principle of the importance of the Constitution and the rule of law to justice and inclusivity for administrative action; the way in which courts have used the Constitution to interpret the limits of administrative discretion as to the process and impacts of decisions; and the application of the administrative oath to uphold the Constitution in the face of political demands to act against the law.

Taking a leaf from Waldo and drawing on the civic republican approach, we may argue that the practice of administration should be expressly based on constitutional goals rather than the pursuit of utilitarian (cost–benefit) or instrumental (cost–effectiveness) forms of efficiency. The constitutional approach opens up the possibility of a separation of powers between the public administrator and the government of the day in which the duty of the public administrator is to the law and constitution and to serve and foster the wider and more inclusive deliberations of the polity.

Constitutional change to the purpose of bureaucracy would represent the ultimate – and likely most challenging – expression of a new approach, shaping as it would all aspects of civic and bureaucratic life. The language of the new constitution would need to draw deeply from existing values and historical traditions that resonate with civil society to create a new regime of truth. Such drafting would clearly be culturally dependent and need to be developed through an extensive process of engagement: it would not be a case of simply borrowing from a Wales or a Bolivia. In the context of the global social and environmental challenges, the constitution would also need directly to address the relationship of the state with the world and our duties to it (as Pettit has suggested in *Justice as Freedom* (Pettit, 2014)). The final text would need to be high level but as coherent, concise and as unambiguous as possible to provide the basis for the 'empire of laws', not a shopping list of incompatible separate goals on differing topics.

Ending this pen portrait of civic bureaucracy with constitutionalism may seem a bridge too far, but constitutions remain the ultimate tool for a transparent reboot of the nature and purpose of governance. Constitutional action can address the structures of political governance to create more localized or communal forms of governance and the ability to represent interests of the non-human world or future generations. A constitution is also where the issue of providing new rights, protections and responsibilities could be addressed. Above all, a constitutional approach would guide both civic bureaucracy and the polity it serves.

Characterizing the new civic bureaucracy

Table 5.3: Practice

Inherited model	Inherited toolkit	New model	New toolkit
Reductionism	Statistics Modelling Forecasting Cost–benefits analysis	Complexity and richness	Deliberation Local decisions Multicriteria analysis
Technocracy	Evidence-based policymaking	Co-production	People-based policymaking Valuing different knowledges
Executive discretion	General discretion of executive	Legal process	Legal process for decision-making and funding
Control	Regulation Finance Audit	Support	Partnership Delegation Dialogue
Targets	Performance indicators Contracts Legal targets	Shared outcomes	Common purpose Peer learning Reflexivity
Economics	Economic models and methods	Values	Broad based, non-positivist methods
Closed	Bounded rationality Confidential or opaque process	Open	Civic engagement Transparency

Table 5.4: Organization

Inherited model	Inherited toolkit	New model	New toolkit
Separation of functions	Topic-based accountabilities and spending	Systems thinking	Goal- and place-based accountabilities, structures and spending
Hierarchy	Management structures	Common purpose	Dialogue structures Heterarchy
Heroic or charismatic leadership	Central strategy Cascade briefing Slogans	Enabling leadership	Emergent strategy Core behaviours Networks
Centralizing	Headquarters Controlling hierarchy	Localizing	Devolved responsibility Local presence
Representative democracy	Formal consultation Serving government	Participative democracy	Inclusive debate and learning Serving people and governance
Competition	Bidding Marketization Consumer choice	Collaboration	Common goals Duty to collaborate Social and public providers Citizen voice

Table 5.5: Purpose and functions

Inherited model	Inherited toolkit	New model	New toolkit
Growth	GNP Market performance	Well-being	Happiness Equality Self-realization 'Main Street'
Conservation	Habitat and species designations	Ecological resilience	Increasing ecological function and health
Regeneration	Physical displacement of communities	Capacity building	Asset-based work with communities Community ownership
Land use planning	Economic agglomeration National infrastructure	Spatial planning	Economic distribution Local infrastructure Community planning
Constitution or common law	Individual freedoms Individual rights	Constitution	Civic rights and duties Legal civic protections
Transitions	Planning Modelling Forecasting	Transformations	Dialogue Systems Reflexivity
Transport	Major hard infrastructure Car-based facilities	Accessibility	Local and soft infrastructure Local facilities

Closing words

A republic – if you can keep it.

Benjamin Franklin

The Brundtland Report called in the late 1980s for a radical new global ethic of sustainable development. This aim has been constrained and co-opted by practice and values drawn from very different views of the way the world and life should work, and it is under challenge from bleak views of society and of civics.

The persistence of existing bureaucratic norms and practices constitute a hidden factor in unsustainability, reinforcing wider political and social norms of governance. By recognizing this, we can begin to scope a new purpose and accompanying processes for public administration. These processes can embed an enabling, systemic and reflexive approach. Much of the basis for this can be found in new approaches being pursued in response to the challenge of reshaping governance to address unsustainability at multiple levels of governance. This practice can find further focus by applying a civic republican approach to change which sees a new basis for governance as non-domination, with dialogue and civic responsibility at its heart.

This book has focused on the role of public bureaucracy. Bureaucracy matters because it shapes what is possible in governance relations and what counts as success. Its repetitive practice and specific disciplines are central to constraining possibilities across the whole system. Foucault's concept of governmentality embraces the notion of power being established in the interplay of relationships. Bureaucracy is a key (and potentially most readily reformable) element in this complex interplay of actors and networks in governance.

Changing bureaucracy is a necessary if not sufficient condition for meaningful change. The cases considered in this book indicate where the interplay of societal expectations, of representative democracy and of market capitalism, serve to limit the scope for reform and reassert traditional narratives. Invoking the spirit of the Brundtland introduction, a new bureaucratic agenda is not a purely technocratic one. It must also be part of, and foster, a societal and political discussion about the purpose of governing and the nature of a just and inclusive democracy in this new century. This includes the perennial question of what government should do, but now posed from a different viewpoint. This is not government juxtaposed with individual freedom and national economic performance but considered against competition from non-democratic models, the decline of civic engagement and trust, the tragedy of the commons, mounting inequalities, and existential threats to environment and health.

Appendices

Appendix 1: Enabling co-productive deliberative democracy in places – a guidance note

Abstracted from: Quinn and de Vrieze (2019)

Understanding place

Why does place matter?
Place links people together

People with different experiences come together in places. Place provides a context in which people have things in common and can interact with each other.

Place links different systems

Places are inherently connected. Social, economic and ecological aspects of life are very visible and the links between them more tangible when viewed from the perspective of place.

Place has meaning

Places have meaning for people. Place can connect individual values and collective identities. Shared sense of place can be a motivation for action.

Place shapes opportunities and barriers

The physical form of places, their infrastructure, ownership and uses shape how we can live our lives and can enable or disable sustainable pathways.

What do we mean by place?
Place is recognisable as a place

There is no set size for what constitutes place but it is usually a combination of a physical identity – a village, small town or landscape, or even a workplace – and a shared social sense of place and identity. Place is at its best as a forum for developing action when there is genuine sense or senses of place and identities.

Place can operate at different scales

A place that makes sense for one issue or question may not for another. The optimum scale or scales for addressing an issue should reflect the needs of the topic and of the likely participants, not what is simplest for the organizer. Often action will be needed at different scales to address an issue.

Place cuts across boundaries of wealth and institutions

Places throw people together. This is part of the power of place as a means of co-producing new approaches. It does not respect boundaries that can otherwise break up an issue into sectoral or administrative divides or favour one group over another

Place makes otherwise abstract ideas real

Place is a real physical case for discussion. The impacts of one decision for other issues or of one group's priorities over another's are tangible and debated in the same room. The physicality of place also determines available options and opportunities

What don't we mean by place?

Places are not defined by administrative boundaries

Places need to be meaningful for people who live there and the issues under discussion. What you may initially view as a place may not be meaningful and can mask differing communities and interests. Be ready to change the place definition or scale. Also be aware of the varying scales at which issues may need to be addressed and plan to engage at appropriate levels and make links between those discussions – what makes sense nationally may seem very different locally and vice versa.

Understanding co-production

Why does co-production matter?

Co-production (sometimes referred to as co-design or social innovation) is a process of combining the practical knowledge and experience of those most affected by an issue with different forms of professional insights in order together to create and deliver something new and shared. It therefore differs significantly from the traditional use of consultation to inform decisions.

Co-production offers elements important for creating sustainable change:

It can help people to **map** how they interact with each other and with their places and see what is important to local well-being

It can **give voice** to a wider range of perspectives and identify local knowledge and priorities in order to create a different understanding of issues and their potential solutions

It can **bring people together** with different experiences and world views, releasing creativity and innovation and building trust and community capacity

What do we mean by co-production?

Co-production is about genuinely sharing power and knowledge

Genuine co-production seeks to put the community at the centre and places professional or institutional roles in a supportive rather than a controlling role. It aims to establish a genuine dialogue that enhances mutual understanding and builds capacity to learn and act together

Co-production is doing *with* not doing *to*

Co-production seeks to reverse the tendency of administrators and experts to know what is best for others without really involving them. Doing *with* people builds the confidence of those engaged and enhances the likely success of the resulting actions.

Co-production regards everyone as having value

This is a fundamental principle of co-production in order to empower people and to show how they can bring insight, contribute, and take control of issues of concern.

Co-production seeks to empower those with least voice

By giving voice to those with little voice in decision-making, co-production improves the decision-making process, increases confidence and self-worth for those participating and helps connect different groups and interests.

Co-production seeks to build new common understanding

By working across divides of expertise and sectors and bringing together people with different interests and understandings, co-production can shape actions to deliver wider and more equal benefits.

What don't we mean by co-production
Co-production isn't holding a consultation workshop

Co-production must give participants the opportunity to determine and shape the debate and the scope to explore and develop ideas. If there is already a decided or firm proposition for whatever reason, be honest about that and engage in normal consultation to understand impacts for different groups.

Co-production isn't about talking to the usual participants

Co-production can't easily be based on existing decision-making groups or policy processes. It needs specific design to reduce the impacts of unequal power and voice among participants and support them to define issues and develop responses.

Co-production isn't about keeping different groups or views separate

One of the powers of co-production, especially when combined with place-based working, is to bring people together rather than treat them as distinct, competing interests. Place-based co-production seeks to bring people together on a basis of equality, though to achieve this you may first need to work with groups separately so as not to disadvantage marginalized voices.

Planning for your participation
Why does preparation matter?

It is very easy to undermine the trust of participants in place-based engagement by being inconsistent or unclear in the approach or application of the basic principles. The success of place-based participation therefore rests in the careful design of the process of engagement and the willingness to be flexible in responding to how the participants wish to shape the work.

What you need to consider
Get the design right

The detailed design of participation will shape the results. Consider how ready or able people are to engage – should different groups be seen separately before bringing people together?; what methods of engagement would give people most equal voice or put them at ease?; are there bridges to build between different interests?; how do you prevent domination by a few voices?; does the situation need independent chairing or facilitation? Above all, always remember to agree the principles and desired outcomes of the process with participants.

Get the people right

In setting up place-based engagement, your first question is whom to involve. This should include all those with an interest or whom the issue will affect. Be careful about relying on proxy representatives of a community or community of interest in case they are unrepresentative of a wider range of views. The richer the debate and engagement the better, as the purpose is increasing understanding, not getting quick consent to a proposal. Be open to adding other voices if others wish it.

Get the methods right

Different groups will thrive in different environments. Traditional policy groups will favour table debate and discussion. Different approaches, such as arts-based participation, can level the playing field, give more equal voice to others and open up new ideas and perspectives rather than play out existing positions. Chose techniques and locations consciously to bring out everyone's creative voice. Be ready to vary and change. Think of ways to bring in other views – for example using images and social media.

Ask a good question

This can be the most difficult issue as the question or issue posed needs to be clear but also open. Too big a question and it is unlikely to be meaningful. Too narrow a question and it is unlikely to be very relevant or interesting. Do not come with pre-formed ideas or proposals to test – let them emerge and be tested in discussion: too often, traditional consultation or engagements have already reached a solution and define the question much too narrowly, preventing fresh insights. Be ready to flex the issue in response to views of initial participants and emerging ideas.

Commit the right time and resources

Time and resources are often in short supply in public administration, but genuine engagement needs a commitment of both. Make clear up front, the commitment of your time and resources and that expected of others and agree how long you want to work together.

Learn together

Co-production is essentially a process of collective learning. This learning needs to be captured, shared and sustained if it is to have lasting impact. Think about and discuss how this can be done at the beginning, through websites, social media, exhibitions, events and storytelling and how that learning will be sustained after the life of the immediate work.

Appendix 2: DESD Senior Managers' Way of Working Charter

Welsh Government departments reacted to the Well-being Act by considering what it meant for change to internal behaviours. The following is an early example of my former Welsh Government department's commitments.

★★★

We will:

Hold regular team meetings to give and receive two-way feedback
Engage people from the start
Be open and honest
Be humble and share our 'half baked' ideas
Identify potentially useful 'foggy' areas/issues and engage on them
Say; 'thank you' about specific actions, face-to-face as soon as we can after the event
Be consistent
Be clear about the rules and stick to them
Reduce the burden of unnecessary bureaucracy
Think first about what's already happening/working and not working here and elsewhere
Respect and respond to other people's priorities
Look for the opportunity and the creative solution
Show or tell people how their feedback has had an impact
Empower and support people to take managed risks together
Apply co-design, co-production and co-delivery as our modus operandi
Work collegiately with wider stakeholders in our programmes and projects
Learn from each other and everyone else

Appendix 3: Written evidence to the Public Accounts committee

The following written evidence was submitted by the lead civil servant of the Welsh Government to a Welsh Senedd Public Accounts Committee inquiry into the Well-being Act. The Committee reported its finding in May 2021, calling for clear cross-society and cross-party support for the implementation of the Act which it commended for its impact on the operation of public services.

★★★

Public Accounts Committee Inquiry | Barriers to the successful implementation of the Well-being of Future Generations (Wales) Act 2015
  Supporting Paper from Permanent Secretary (Welsh Government) 15 January 2021

Introduction

The Welsh Government has a long history of promoting sustainable development and committing to making sustainable development the central organising principle of government. The fact that this is not new for us is a strength, but expectations are much higher as a result of the Well-being of Future Generations Act, particularly as governance structures and accountability should be considerably strengthened by the legislation.

The role of the Welsh Government civil service under the Well-being of Future Generations (Wales) Act 2015 ('the WFG Act') is to support Welsh Ministers in discharging their duties under the Act and delivering their well-being objectives, as well as their promotion of sustainable development. The legislation is designed to make sustainable development the central organising principle of government and public bodies, and it follows that the operation, governance and mechanics of Government, and the advice and support provided by the Welsh civil service should continually improve to respond to these requirements.

This supporting paper has been prepared in advance of the scrutiny of Welsh Government officials on 1 February 2021 by the Public Accounts Committee. The paper therefore focuses on the actions I have taken as Permanent Secretary with the Executive Committee and officials from across the Welsh Government.

This paper will not cover those policy matters that are for Welsh Ministers. In 2017, the Welsh Government published 12 well-being objectives as required by the WFG Act, which were included in Prosperity for all: the national strategy. The government's Annual Report 2019 outlines the progress made against these objectives under the First Ministers' three themes of 'more prosperous, equal, and greener'. The next annual report is due to be published in January 2021 and, in accordance with Standing Order 11.21(ii) the Welsh Government is due to propose a debate on the Programme for Government Annual Report in February 2021.

Implementation by the Welsh civil service Since the WFG Act came into force in 2017 the sustainable development principle and well-being duty has affected every aspect of our organisational operating model, from our policy-making framework, our performance management; our leadership expectations; and our financial and auditing processes. It has also provided the foundation for my future-proofing initiative. Through the Welsh Government Consolidated Accounts, I provide an annual summary of actions taken to further embed the sustainable development principle in how we work. Over the course of this government term, stakeholders have constructively challenged Welsh Ministers and the civil service about the pace of change in embedding the WFG Act and the culture change it requires. The latest accounts published in November 2020, describe how we reflected on how we were co-ordinating our response to the WFG Act, and agreed to an updated strategic implementation framework to better reflect and communicate the breadth and scope of the WFG Act within Government. This framework, importantly distinguishes the

- ❏ the role of Welsh Ministers in maximising Government's contribution to the well-being goals by setting and delivering well-being objectives;
- ❏ the role of the Civil Service in improving the support and advice to Welsh Ministers by embedding the sustainable development principle in how we work;
- ❏ our role in enabling others to contribute to the achievement of the well-being goals and implement the WFG Act; and,
- ❏ our role in helping to understand Wales now and in the future through work on the future trends report, national well-being indicators and Annual Wellbeing of Wales report.

In the early phase of implementation of the WFG Act, the Welsh Government worked with stakeholders to develop and deliver key building blocks to support successful national implementation of the WFG Act duties. These include; the statutory guidance for public bodies, Public Services Boards and community councils; the national wellbeing indicators measuring the progress towards the well-being goals laid before the Senedd in 2016; the first statutory Welsh Government Future Trends Report in 2017; and the first Annual Well-being of Wales Report by the Chief Statistician in September 2017. In addition, we have provided a range of resources to help raise awareness and understanding of the WFG Act, for example, an easy read document, essentials guide and animation, and explainers of how the WFG Act links to other legislation. These complement the work of the Future Generations Commissioner and her team who play a pivotal role in supporting national implementation.

Within the Welsh Government, each policy and portfolio area is responsible for embedding the sustainable development principle into its activities, policies and arrangements, and for taking action to deliver the Government's stated well-being objectives. We recognised the need for the centre of the organisation to oversee and enable the change. Early work on internal implementation the WFG Act focused on establishing and ensuring the delivery of key internal actions to facilitate compliance and an understanding of the aspirations behind the legislation to all staff. We focused on changes to our operations and business processes; engaging staff and facilitating behaviour change; with a look to the wider One Welsh Public service and our enabling role.

Our work with WWF Cymru in 2017/18 helped to forge a common understanding with stakeholders of how Welsh Government's progress in operating under the WFG Act can be seen, understood, and recognised. Through a series of workshops, pointers for action were identified and published in 'All Together' (2018). In my foreword to the report I welcomed co-productive spirit in which officials and third sector representatives tackled the issues on implementation. Our continued engagement with the Auditor General, Audit Wales and the Future Generations Commissioner has also provided ongoing feedback and learning on how we respond to the WFG Act.

Engaging staff and facilitating behaviour change

I recognise that the Act is fundamentally about changing behaviours and how decisions are made. The kind of sustained behaviour change expected by the legislation and sustainable development agenda takes time, and requires continual improvements in how we lead; how we learn; how we perform; and, how we work. These elements form the basis of my future-proofing initiative, which was designed at the outset to equip the Welsh civil service to meet the challenges of delivering the WFG Act. It differs from previous change programmes (including 'Preparing for the Future') in its deliberate focus on people-related change and the integrated and system-wide nature of the way we are approaching the behaviour change programme. To raise awareness in the civil service of the WFG Act we developed a core narrative; ran a series of workshop sessions with the entire Senior Civil Service; delivered preparing for the future roadshow events; delivered resource packs for staff and a new intranet resource area. Deep dive events were also run on each of the five ways of working for the policy profession. Policy making and ministerial advice guidance was all updated to ensure considerations of the Act formed part of this work, and we keep this under review. We also developed a common communication toolkit with heads of internal communications across the public sector. When we recruit, we expect candidates to have knowledge and understanding of the Act. We know that from our People Survey in 2020 there appears to be relatively high levels of initial adoption of the five ways of working. In 2021 we will be exploring this adoption further through an internal audit exercise of Departments to identify and share good practice.

Changes to our operations and business processes

We recognised that our processes and mechanisms could be a driver for implementing the WFG Act, particularly the five ways of working. Early achievements included embedding the WFG Act into business planning, looking at integration of impact, the role of the Internal Control mechanisms and governance statement; and, amendments to remit letters and grant conditions. In support of the Minister for Finance and Trefnydd, we worked with the third sector and the Future Generations Commissioner to agree a multi-layered definition of prevention.

A Well-being of Future Generations (WFG) Champion has been appointed to lead WFG considerations on the Welsh Government Board, and a revised Terms of Reference emphasises its role in providing strategic advice in line with the WFG Act.

The Board Champion also leads the WFG Oversight and Enabling Group, a cross government group comprising those responsible for statutory or operationally important elements of Welsh Government duties and responsibilities under the Act. To support policy integration and coherence a process was put in place for key Cabinet papers with 'challenge sessions' held with Welsh Government officials, as papers are developed to ensure a cross government approach to policy making. My approach to these sessions were informed by regular conversations with the Future Generations Commissioner so that lines of inquiry were developed that focused on the five ways of working. The lessons from these challenge sessions have now been fed into a dedicated Delivery Board. The Delivery Board scrutinises delivery of our government priorities through a collective lens, ensuring that Government can contribute to the achievement of the well-being goals through collaboration and cross-government action.

One Welsh Public Service and enabling others

The One Welsh Public Service (OWPS) ethos has a shared purpose and shared drivers to achieve a better and lasting quality of life for all, designed around the outcomes of the WFG Act, the five ways of working and the public service values we hold.

The Academi Wales website provides resources for public service leaders and promotes a series of masterclasses and workshops which support the OWPS ethos and support the WFG Act. Academi Wales highlight their main achievements through their Annual Report.

Academi Wales delivered a number of modules on the first cohort of the Future Generations Leadership Academy programme, designed by the Future Generations Commissioner office and Academi Wales to build the leadership skills of younger members of the public service, who will one day become the leaders of future generations. Academi Wales will continue to provide support for future cohorts. The second planned intake of the All Wales Public Service Graduate Programme, commencing in January 2022 will be open to public/ third sector partners and will require organisations to demonstrate collaboration within a region and illustrate how their projects support the concept of OWPS; the Well-being of Future Generations Act and regional priorities. We further recognise the good practice across Wales delivered in many different ways. For example, for the Ystadau Cymru Awards and the All Wales Continuous Improvement (AWCIC) Awards, the Well-being of Future Generations Act five ways of working was used to inform the nomination process highlighting the improvement work being carried out in public services and third sector organisations across Wales. Both awards include categories recognising teams and organisations applying the WFG Act in their work.

In January 2020, we delivered the first Future Generations Xchange event which brought together senior managers across the Civil Service and wider public sector to share practice in applying the five ways of working. Over 300 people attended which included a keynote address from the First Minister. We will be building on the success of this event, and continue to provide opportunities for staff to come together and discuss better ways of working in 2021.

The Committee will be aware of the wide-ranging review of our sponsorship arrangements that we commissioned in 2018 ('Delivering Together – Strengthening the Welsh Government's Sponsorship of Arms-length bodies'). This included recommendations which emphasise the ability of the Welsh Government and its arms-length bodies to work together in ways which are consistent with the WFG Act.

Our Framework Document sets out the relationship between Welsh Government Sponsored Bodies and Ministers, including roles and responsibilities, and the terms and conditions under which we pay them grant in aid. This document, and remit letters include strong references and messages to those bodies to ensure their work contributes to the WFG agenda, employing the five ways of working, reporting on WFG matters and are linked to the Welsh Governments well-being objectives.

In 2019 we worked with stakeholders to input into the UK Government's Voluntary National Review of the Sustainable Development Goals to ensure Wales' approach was strongly featured, we also drafted and published a separate 'Wales and the Sustainable Development Goals'. This provided a review of Wales' contribution to the Sustainable Development Goals and agenda through the framework of the WFG Act. Building on this we worked in partnership with the Institute for Advance Sustainability Studies in Germany to deliver an international event, 'The Future is Now' in March 2020.

In May 2020, Welsh Government joined the Wellbeing Economy Government (WEGo) network alongside Scotland, Iceland and New Zealand. Since joining the WEGo network earlier in the year, Welsh Government officials have derived great benefit form hearing about the experiences of other governments in applying the principles of well-being economics. We have also been able to share our own experiences of developing policy in the context of the ground-breaking Future Generations Act and particularly in monitoring our progress against the well-being goals established in the Act, using the broad indicator set developed to capture the multiple dimensions of well-being.

Views on the barriers to implementation

The responses to the PAC consultation and the reports of the Auditor General and Future Generations Commissioner have highlighted a number of potential barriers and opportunities to the implementation of the WFG Act. I want to outline the work we have been doing to understand and address some of the key barriers.

Funding arrangements

The WFG Act seeks to ensure that Welsh Government and public bodies take greater account of the long-term impact of the things they do, and to plan accordingly. This can understandably be challenging when financial certainty can only be given for short periods. Welsh Ministers have indicated their desire to be in a position to provide longer-term financial certainty, however are only able to set revenue and capital plans for a single year due to UK Government spending decisions. We will continue to press for longer financial settlements. In terms of infrastructure investment, we are working on a whole government approach to enhance connections across portfolios and maximise the public returns on investment. Following the 'Delivering Together' work in 2018 we are exploring how we could move away from annual remit letters, budget awards and business plans to a 'Term of Government' approach to enable longer term planning for our arms-length bodies.

Partnership landscape

The importance of collaboration between different organisations delivering for people and the environment is an essential ingredient for sustainable development. The WFG Act recognized this and included collaboration as one of the five ways of working for public bodies to take into account. This way of working was strengthened further by establishing formal collaborative arrangements through Public Services Boards. We have provided support to Public Services Boards since their establishment through network meetings, workshops, 'drop-in' clinics, and regional funding for activities. These have supported their capacity and capability to develop local assessments of well-being, well-being plans and also delivery against those plans. Senior Civil Servants are members of each board and have terms of reference for their role as invited attendees on behalf of Welsh Ministers. The role of the Welsh Government representative is to bring a national perspective to meetings and to ensure that national and regional delivery remains responsive to local issues and local democratic accountability.

Public Services Boards sit within a wider landscape of partnership arrangements. In recognition of a mutual problem, that of simplifying complexities in Welsh public services working together, a review of strategic partnerships was conducted with the Welsh Local Government Association and Welsh NHS Confederation. The Review of Strategic Partnerships reported in June to the Partnership Council for Wales. Whilst there was agreement that the partnership landscape is complex, the review found little support for uniform removal or merger of partnerships – either by partnership theme or area. Partnership Council agreed a pragmatic solution based on local leadership, which Welsh Government will facilitate.

Legislative landscape

The nature of the WFG Act means that new Bills that look to change the way that public bodies operate may interact with the duties in the WFG Act. Our Legislation Handbook reminds officials that when developing legislation that they should consider whether the proposed legislation will contribute to the delivery of the Act.

We also published Making Good Decisions in 2016 to assist public authorities in Wales to make good decisions that are lawful and comply with the Rule of Law. In developing new legislation, we have looked for opportunities to clarify their relationship with existing legislation, such as the Planning (Wales) Act 2015; the Environment (Wales) Act 2016; the Social Services and Well-being (Wales) Act 2014; the Local Government and Elections (Wales) Act 2021; and, the draft tertiary Education and Research Bill. More recently, we have worked with the Equality and Human Rights Commission Wales and the Future Generations Commissioner to develop guidance to help public bodies consider opportunities to apply the socioeconomic, the public sector equality and the well-being of future generations' duties in an aligned way.

Reporting

The reporting requirements for the WFG Act are designed to be a vehicle for organisations to communicate how they are contributing to the well-being goals and carrying out sustainable development. The statutory guidance encourages public bodies and Public Services Boards to report on progress through existing mechanisms, such as existing annual reporting mechanisms rather than in isolation from other reporting activities. The guidance advocates an integrated reporting approach and encourages bodies to explore opportunities to integrate the way in which they report existing duties.

Looking ahead

The reports from the Future Generations Commissioner and Auditor General for Wales, as well as the work we have done with the third sector provides an array of ideas for how the Welsh Government civil service can realise the benefits of working in a more sustainable way. In early 2020 the Executive Committee discussed the internal barriers to realising the benefits of the legislation. These covered aspects such as improving joined up government; using the Future Trends Report as a platform to build capacity for long term thinking; embedding a preventative approach beyond the budget; and how we can improve the capability of our policy profession.

We also acknowledged the importance for Welsh Government to show visible leadership and improve how we communicate the changes we are making. I identified a series of additional actions to take to embed the sustainable development principle in the workings of the Civil Service. I will be attending the Caerphilly Public Services Board in January 2021, and have convened a meeting of the Welsh Government officials on PSBs in January as part of a bi-annual session to exchange information and improve our leadership role on PSBs.

Appendix 4: Extracts from UK civil service code

As a civil servant, you are appointed on merit on the basis of fair and open competition and are expected to carry out your role with dedication and a commitment to the Civil Service and its core values: integrity, honesty, objectivity and impartiality. In this code:

- 'integrity' is putting the obligations of public service above your own personal interests
- 'honesty' is being truthful and open
- 'objectivity' is basing your advice and decisions on rigorous analysis of the evidence
- 'impartiality' is acting solely according to the merits of the case and serving equally well governments of different political persuasions

These core values support good government and ensure the achievement of the highest possible standards in all that the Civil Service does. This in turn helps the Civil Service to gain and retain the respect of ministers, Parliament, the public and its customers.

Integrity

You must:

- fulfil your duties and obligations responsibly
- always act in a way that is professional and that deserves and retains the confidence of all those with whom you have dealings
- carry out your fiduciary obligations responsibly (that is make sure public money and other resources are used properly and efficiently)
- deal with the public and their affairs fairly, efficiently, promptly, effectively and sensitively, to the best of your ability
- ensure you have Ministerial authorisation for any contact with the media
- keep accurate official records and handle information as openly as possible within the legal framework
- comply with the law and uphold the administration of justice

You must not:

- misuse your official position, for example by using information acquired in the course of your official duties to further your private interests or those of others

- accept gifts or hospitality or receive other benefits from anyone which might reasonably be seen to compromise your personal judgement or integrity
- disclose official information without authority (this duty continues to apply after you leave the Civil Service)

Honesty

You must:

- set out the facts and relevant issues truthfully, and correct any errors as soon as possible
- use resources only for the authorised public purposes for which they are provided

You must not:

- deceive or knowingly mislead ministers, Parliament or others
- be influenced by improper pressures from others or the prospect of personal gain

Objectivity

You must:

- provide information and advice, including advice to ministers, on the basis of the evidence, and accurately present the options and facts
- take decisions on the merits of the case
- take due account of expert and professional advice

You must not:

- ignore inconvenient facts or relevant considerations when providing advice or making decisions
- frustrate the implementation of policies once decisions are taken by declining to take, or abstaining from, action which flows from those decisions

Impartiality

You must:

- carry out your responsibilities in a way that is fair, just and equitable and reflects the Civil Service commitment to equality and diversity

You must not:

- act in a way that unjustifiably favours or discriminates against particular individuals or interests

Political Impartiality

You must:

- serve the government, whatever its political persuasion, to the best of your ability in a way which maintains political impartiality and is in line with the requirements of this code, no matter what your own political beliefs are
- act in a way which deserves and retains the confidence of ministers, while at the same time ensuring that you will be able to establish the same relationship with those whom you may be required to serve in some future government
- comply with any restrictions that have been laid down on your political activities

You must not:

- act in a way that is determined by party political considerations, or use official resources for party political purposes
- allow your personal political views to determine any advice you give or your actions.

Appendix 5: Interview format

Exploring learning from Wales' experience of governing for sustainable development

The stated purpose of the Well-being of Future Generations Act was 'to govern for sustainable development'. This research seeks to identify learning from the Welsh experience as to the implications of governing for sustainable development for existing practices of government, with practices defined broadly to include rules, norms, behaviours, values, narratives, institutions, organisation, processes and systems. The research aims to identify the key opportunities, tensions and barriers revealed by the Welsh experience of seeking to govern for sustainable development since devolution in 1998. In the context of the UN Sustainable Development Goals and in what has been described as our present 'turbulent age', we explore what insights the Welsh experience can bring to current practices of government and how they may need to evolve to address 21st-century challenges.

Q1 State your name and briefly set out what roles you've had in relation to governing for sustainable development in the period 1998 to present.

Q2 Based on your experience, what do you see as the key elements or characteristics of governing for sustainable development?

Q3 Tell me in as much detail as you can recall of occasions when you encountered specific tensions between existing practices of government and governing for Sustainable Development (examples will be anonymised in any reporting). Might be an idea to start chronologically?

[I'll suggest some specific areas of practice to consider if we stall (prompt list attached below)]

Q4 Of the examples we've discussed, what solutions or opportunities were found to move things on, and which practices remained as persistent barriers?

Q5 Why do you feel the remaining barriers you identified persisted?

Q6 Anything else you think would be of interest in the context of the study?

[Subheadings as potential prompts/ checklist for interview coverage]

Institutions

Departmental/ministerial structures
Individual institutions and their separate remits

Legislative–executive separation
Multilevel governance
Representative democracy
Political parties
Media

Processes

Grant giving
Business cases
Options appraisal and assessments
Objective setting and KPIs
Managerialism
Procurement
Commissioning
Targets
Evaluation
Recruitment
Public appointments

Rules

Accountability for ministerial budgets and actions
Civil service code
Legal privilege
UK law conventions

Dominant/absent narratives

Public policy priorities
Agenda setting
What is and is not legitimate for action
Memes, sayings and truisms
Public services
Central vs local
Community or individual

Professional frames/methods

Economics
Statistics
Land use planning

Health profession
Engineering
Comms
Political
Other

Emotions and beliefs

Responses to SD from different perspectives?
People characteristics and behaviours

References

Alford, J. (2014) 'The multiple facets of co-production: Building on the work of Elinor Ostrom', *Public Management Review*, 16(3): 299–316.

Alwaer, H. and Cooper, I. (2019) 'A review of the role of facilitators in community-based, design-led planning and placemaking events', *Built Environment*, 45(2): 190–211.

Anderson, V. (2018) *Protecting the Interests of Future Generations*, CUSP Working Paper (14), Guildford: University of Surrey.

Andonova, L.B. and Levy, M.A. (2003) 'Franchising global governance: Making sense of the Johannesburg type II partnerships', in Stokke, O.S. and Thommesson, O.B. (eds) *Yearbook of International Co-operation on Environment and Development 2003/2004*, London: Earthscan, 19–31.

Ang, F. and Passel, S.V. (2012) 'Beyond the environmentalist's paradox and the debate on weak versus strong sustainability', *BioScience*, 62(3): 251–9.

Arendt, H. (2003) *The Portable Hannah Arendt*, Baehr, P. (ed), New York: Penguin Books.

Armstrong, R. (1985) 'Written answer by the prime minister to a parliamentary question on 26 February 1985', *Hansard, HC Deb*, vol 74, cc 128–130.

Auld, E. and Morris, P. (2016) 'PISA, policy and persuasion: Translating complex conditions into education "best practice"', *Comparative Education*, 52(2): 202–29.

Baker, S. (2007) 'Sustainable development as symbolic commitment: Declaratory politics and the seductive appeal of ecological modernisation in the European Union', *Environmental Politics*, 16(2): 297–317.

Baker, S. (2012) 'Climate change, the common good and the promotion of sustainable development', in Meadowcroft, J., Langhelle, O. and Ruud, A. (eds) *Governance, Democracy and Sustainable Development Moving Beyond the Impasse*, Cheltenham: Edward Elgar, 249–271.

Baker, S. (2016) *Sustainable Development*, 2nd edn, Abingdon and New York: Routledge.

Baker, S. and Durance, I. (2018) 'Resilience and adaptation in natural-social systems: A place-based perspective', in T. Marsden (ed) *The Sage Handbook of Nature*, London: Sage, 370–91.

Barry, J. (2008) 'Towards a green republicanism: Constitutionalism, political economy, and the green state', *The Good Society*, 17(2): 3–11.

Barry, J. (2012) *The Politics of Actually Existing Unsustainability: Human Flourishing in a Climate-changed, Carbon Constrained World*, Oxford: Oxford University Press.

Bauer, R. (2019) *The Peasant Production of Opium in Nineteenth-century India*, Leiden and Boston: Brill.

References

BBC Wales (2021) 'Climate Change: Carwyn Jones defends his record as he leaves the Senedd', 23 May. https://www.bbc.co.uk/news/uk-wales-57204249.amp

Beer, D. (2016) *Metric Power*, Basingstoke: Palgrave Macmillan.

Bergh, J.C.J.M. (2011) 'Environment versus growth: A criticism of "degrowth" and a plea for "a-growth"', *Ecological Economics*, 70(5): 881–90.

Berlin, I. (1969) 'Two concepts of liberty', in *Four Essays on Liberty*, Oxford: Oxford University Press 118–172.

Bertrand, F. (2005) 'Aménagement du territoire et développement durable', in M. Bonnard, *Les collectivités territoriales en France*, Paris: la Documentation française, 136–42.

Bevir, M. (2010) *Democratic Governance*, Princeton and Woodstock: Princeton University Press.

Blühdorn, I. and Welsh, I. (eds) (2008) *The Politics of Unsustainability: Eco-politics in the Post-ecologist Era*, London: Routledge.

Boyd, D.R. (2012) *The Environmental Rights Revolution: A Global Study of Constitutions, Human Rights, and the Environment*, Vancouver: UBC Press.

Boyne, G.A. (2003) 'Sources of public service improvement: A critical review and research agenda', *Journal of Public Administration Research and Theory*, 13(3): 367–94.

Brandt, W. (1980) *North-South: A Programme for Survival: Independent Commission on International Development Issues*, London: Pan.

Brown, P.R. and Head, B.W. (2019) 'Navigating tensions in co-production: A missing link in leadership for public value', *Public Administration*, 97(2): 250–63.

Cameron, M.A. (2018) *Political Institutions and Practical Wisdom: Between Rules and Practice*, New York: Oxford University Press.

Canal & River Trust (2017) *Waterways & Wellbeing Building the Evidence Base: First Outcomes Report*, Milton Keynes: Canal & River Trust.

Christensen, T. and Lægreid, P. (2007) *Transcending New Public Management: The Transformation of Public Sector Reforms*, Abingdon: Routledge.

Cook, B.J. (2007) *Democracy and Administration: Woodrow Wilson's Ideas and the Challenges of Public Management*, Baltimore: Johns Hopkins University Press.

Dalrymple, W. (2019) *The Anarchy: The Relentless Rise of the East India Company*, London: Bloomsbury.

Davidson, J. (2020), *#futuregen Lessons from a Small Country*, Chelsea, VT: Chelsea Green Publishing.

Davies, N. and Williams, D. (2009) *Clear Red Water: Welsh Devolution and Socialist Politics*, London: Francis Boutle.

Death, C. (2010) *Governing Sustainable Development: Partnerships, Protests and Power at the World Summit*, Abingdon and New York: Routledge.

Denhardt, J.V. and Denhardt, R.B. (2007) *The New Public Service Serving, Not Steering*, expanded edn, Armonk: M.E. Sharpe.

Denhardt, J.V. and Denhardt, R.B. (2015) 'The new public service revisited', *Public Administration Review*, 75(5): 664–72.

Desrosières, A. (2002) *The Politics of Large Numbers, a History of Statistical Reasoning*, Cambridge, MA: Harvard University Press.

Dobson, A. (2007) *Green Political Thought*, 4th edn, London: Routledge.

Dreijmanis, J. and Wells, G.C. (2008) *Max Weber's Complete Writings on Academic and Political Vocations*, New York: Algora Publishing.

Dryzek, J.S. (2005) 'Designs for environmental discourse revisited: A greener administrative state?', in Paehlke, R. and Torgerson, D. (eds) *Managing Leviathan: Environmental Politics and the Administrative State*, 2nd edn, Toronto: University of Toronto Press, 81–96.

Dryzek, J.S. (2010) *Foundations and Frontiers of Deliberative Governance*, Oxford: Oxford University Press.

Dryzek, J.S. and Pickering, J. (2019) *The Politics of the Anthropocene*, Oxford: Oxford University Press.

Earth System Governance Project (2018) *Earth System Governance: Science and Implementation Plan of the Earth System Governance Project*, Utrecht.

Eckersley, R. (2004) *The Green State: Rethinking Democracy and Sovereignty*, Cambridge, MA: MIT Press.

Entwistle, T., Bristow, G., Hines, F., Donaldson, S. and Martin, S. (2007) 'The dysfunctions of markets, hierarchies and networks in the meta-governance of partnership', *Urban Studies*, 44(1): 63–79.

Eversole, R. (2012) 'Remaking participation', *Community Development Journal*, 47(1): 29–41.

Fischer, F. (2003) *Reframing Public Policy: Discursive Politics and Deliberative Practices*, New York: Oxford University Press.

Folke, C., Hahn, T., Olsson, P. and Norberg, J. (2005) 'Adaptive governance of social-ecological systems', *Annual Review of Environment and Resources*, 30(1): 441–73.

Fornet-Betancourt, R., Becker, H. and Gomez-Mueller, G. (1987) 'The ethic of care for the self as a practice of freedom: An interview with Michel Foucault on January 20, 1984', *Philosophy & Social Criticism*, 12(2–3): 112–31.

Foucault, M. (1977) 'The political function of the intellectual', *Radical Philosophy*, RP017: 12–14.

Foucault, M. (1991) 'Governmentality', in G. Burchell, C. Gordon, and P. Miller, *The Foucault Effect – Studies in Governmentality with 2 lectures by and an Interview with Michel Foucault*, Chicago: University of Chicago Press, 87–104.

Foucault, M. (2008) *The Birth of Biopolitics: Lectures at the Collège de France, 1978–79*, Cheltenham: Palgrave Macmillan.

Foundational Economy Collective (2018) *Foundational Economy: The Infrastructure of Everyday Life*, Manchester: Manchester University Press.

References

Francis, D. (2002) *People, Peace and Power: Conflict Transformation in Action*, London and Sterling: Pluto Press.

Getha-Taylor, H. (2019) *Partnerships that Last: Identifying the Keys to Resilient Collaboration*, Cambridge: Cambridge University Press.

Getha-Taylor, H., Holmes, M.H., Jacobson, W.S., Morse, R.S. and Sowa, J.E. (2011) 'Focusing the public leadership lens: Research propositions and questions in the Minnowbrook tradition', *Journal of Public Administration Research and Theory*, 21(1): i83–i97.

Goodin, R.E. (1996) 'Institutions and their design', in Goodin R.E. (ed) *Theories of Institutional Design*, Cambridge: Cambridge University Press, 1–53.

Grenni, S., Soini, K. and Horlings, L. (2020) 'The inner dimension of sustainability transformation: How sense of place and values can support sustainable placeshaping', *Sustainability Science*, 15(2): 411–22.

Habermas, J. (1987) *The Theory of Communicative Action, Vol. 2: Lifeworld and System: A Critique of Functionalist Reason*, McCarthy, T. (trans), Cambridge: Polity Press.

Hamilton, A., Madison, J. and Jay, J. (2009) *The Federalist Papers*, Ian Shapiro (ed), New Haven: Yale University Press.

Happaerts, S. (2012) 'Sustainable development in Quebec and Flanders: Institutionalizing symbolic politics?', *Canadian Public Administration*, 55(4): 553–73.

Harmon, M.M. (1989) 'The Simon/Waldo debate: A review and update', *Public Administration Quarterly*, 12(4): 437–51.

Harney, S. (2002) *State Work: Public Administration and Mass Intellectuality*, Durham, NC: Duke University Press.

Harrington, J. (1656) *The Common-wealth of Oceana*, London: Printed by J. Streater for Livewell Chapman.

Hart, L. (1997) *Asset Base Development for Community-based Regeneration Organisations*, London: Development Trusts Association.

Heath, J. (2020) *The Machinery of Government: Public Administration and the Liberal State*, Oxford: Oxford University Press.

Healey, P. (2005) *Collaborative Planning: Shaping Places in Fragmented Societies*, 2nd ed.; London and New York: Palgrave Macmillan.

Heywood, A. (2016) *Local Housing, Community Living: Prospects for Scaling Up and Scaling Out Community-Led Housing*, London: The Smith Institute.

Hobbes, T. (2005) *Leviathan*, Rogers G.A.J. and Schuhmann. K. (eds.,) London: Thoemmes Continuum.

Hoffman, J. (2010) *The Cooperation Challenge of Economics and the Protection of Water Supplies: A Case Study of the New York City Watershed Collaboration*, London: Routledge.

Holling, C.S. (2001) 'Understanding the complexity of economic, ecological and social systems', *Ecosystems*, 4(5): 390–405.

Hood, C. (1991) 'A public management for all seasons?', *Public Administration*, 69(1): 3–19.

Horlings, L., Roep, D., Mathijs, E. and Marsden, T. (2020) 'Exploring the transformative capacity of place-shaping practices', *Sustainability Science*, 15(2): 353–62.

Jackson, T. (2009) *Prosperity without Growth: Economics for a Finite Planet*, Abingdon: Routledge.

Jennings, B. (2016) *Ecological Governance: Towards a New Social Contract with the Earth*, Morgantown: West Virginia University Press.

Kauffman, C.M. and Martin, P.L. (2017) 'Can rights of nature make development more sustainable? Why some Ecuadorian lawsuits succeed and others fail', *World Development*, 92: 130–42.

Kavanagh, D. and Richards, D. (2001) 'Departmentalism and joined-up government', *Parliamentary Affairs*, 54(1): 1–18.

Kelsall, R.K. (1955) *Higher Civil Servants in Britain: From 1870 to the Present Day*, London: Routledge & Kegan Paul Ltd.

Kolodny, A. (1975) *The Lay of the Land: Metaphor as Experience and History in American Life and Letters*, Chapel Hill: University of North Carolina Press.

Koltko-Rivera, M.E. (2004) 'The psychology of worldviews', *Review of General Psychology*, 8(1): 3–58.

Lafferty, W.M. (2012) 'Governance for sustainable development: The impasse of dysfunctional democracy', in Meadowcroft, J., Langhelle, O. and Ruud, A. (eds) *Governance, Democracy and Sustainable Development Moving Beyond the Impasse*, Cheltenham: Edward Elgar: 297–337.

Lang, M. and Marsden, T. (2018) 'Rethinking growth: Towards the well-being economy', *Local Economy*, 33(5): 496–514.

Lascoumes, P. and Le Gales, P. (2007) 'Introduction: Understanding public policy through its instruments—from the nature of instruments to the sociology of public policy instrumentation', *Governance*, 20(1): 1–21.

Lincoln, Y.S. and Guba, E.G. (1985) *Naturalistic Inquiry*, Newbury Park and London: Sage Publications.

Loorbach, D. (2007) *Transition Management: New Modes of Governance for Sustainable Development*, Utrecht: International Books.

Lowe, R. (2011) 'The Northcote-Trevelyan report and the evolution of the civil service 1854–1916', in R. Lowe, *The Official History of the British Civil Service*, London and New York: Routledge, 33–57.

Marx, K. (1970[1843]) *Critique of Hegel's 'Philosophy of Right'*, Jolin, A. and O'malley, J. (trans), New York: Cambridge University Press.

Mayo, A. (1977) *The Human Problems of an Industrial Civilization*, New York: Arno Press.

McNeill, J.R. (2014) *The Great Acceleration: An Environmental History of the Anthropocene since 1945*, Cambridge, MA: Harvard University Press.

Meadowcroft, J. (2007) 'Who is in charge here? Governance for sustainable development in a complex world', *Journal of Environmental Policy & Planning*, 9(3–4): 299–314.

Meadowcroft, J., Langhelle, O. and Ruud, A. (eds) (2012) *Governance, Democracy and Sustainable Development Moving Beyond the Impasse*, Cheltenham: Edward Elgar.

Meadows, D.H. (1972) *The Limits to Growth: A Report for the Club of Rome's Project on the Predicament of Mankind*, London: Earth Island.

Meadows, T.T. (1847) *Desultory Notes on the Government and People of China and on the Chinese Language*, London: Allen & Co.

Mill, J.S. (1965) 'Principles of political economy', in J. M. Robson (ed) *The Collected Works of John Stuart Mill Volume II*, Toronto: University of Toronto Press.

Miller, C.L. (2011) *Implementing Sustainability: The New Zealand Experience*, Abingdon and New York: Routledge.

Mills, C.W. (1959) *The Sociological Imagination*, New York: Oxford University Press.

Montambeault, F. (2015) *The Politics of Local Participatory Democracy in Latin America: Institutions, Actors, and Interactions*, Palo Alto: Stanford University Press.

Montesquieu (1949) *The Spirit of the Laws*, Nugent, T. (trans), New York: Hafner.

Montgomery, T (2015) *Prosperity for All: Restoring Faith in Capitalism*, London: The Legatum Institute.

National Assembly (2000) *Learning to Live Differently: The Sustainable Development Scheme of the National Assembly for Wales*, Cardiff: National Assembly for Wales.

National Assembly (2004) *Starting to Live Differently: The Sustainable Development Scheme of the National Assembly for Wales*, Cardiff: National Assembly for Wales.

National Assembly (2014) *Transcript of the Environment and Sustainability Committee Meeting*, 25 September, [32]. https://business.senedd.wales/documents/s31492/25%20September%202014.pdf

Newbold, S.P. (2010) 'Toward a Constitutional School for American Public Administration', *Public Administration Review*, 70(4): 538–46.

Niskanen, W.A. (1971) *Bureaucracy and Representative Government*, Chicago: Aldine.

Nokkala, E.P. (2009) 'The machine of state in Germany: The case of Johann Heinrich Gottlob von Justi (1717–1771)', *Contributions to the History of Concepts*, 5(1): 71–93.

NRW, (2020) *State of Natural Resources Report (SoNaRR) for Wales 2020.* https://naturalresources.wales/evidence-and-data/research-and-reports/state-of-natural-resources-report-sonarr-for-wales-2020/?lang=en

Osborne, S.P. (2010) *The New Public Governance? Emerging Perspectives on the Theory and Practice of Public Governance*, London: Routledge.

Osborne, S.P. (2020) *Public Service Logic: Creating Value for Public Service Users, Citizens and Society Through Public Service Delivery*, London and New York: Routledge.

Osmond, J. (ed) (1998) *The National Assembly Agenda: A Handbook for the First Four Years*, Cardiff: Institute of Welsh Affairs.

Ostrom, E. (2009) 'A general framework for analyzing sustainability of social-ecological systems', *Science*, 325(5939): 419–22.

Ostrom, E. (2010) 'Beyond markets and states: Polycentric governance of complex economic systems', *American Economic Review*, 100(3): 1–33.

Ostrom, V. and Ostrom, E. (1977) 'Public goods and public choices', in Savas, E.S. (ed) *Alternatives for Delivering Public Services: Toward Improved Performance*, Boulder: Westview Press, 6-49.

Owens, S. and Cowell, R. (2002) *Land and Limits: Interpreting Sustainability in the Planning Process*, London: Routledge.

Oxford English Dictionary (2015) *Third Edition*, Oxford: Oxford University Press.

Panchamia, N. and Thomas, P. (2014) *Civil Service Reform in the Real World: Patterns of Success in UK Civil Service Reform*, London: Institute for Government.

Patterson, J., Schulz, K., Vervoort, J., van der Hel, S., Widerberg, O., Adler, C., Hurlbert, M., Anderton, K., Sethi, M. and Barau, A. (2017) 'Exploring the governance and politics of transformations towards sustainability', *Environmental Innovation and Societal Transitions*, 24: 1–16.

Pearce, D., Markandya, A. and Barbier, E.B. (1989) *Blueprint for a Green Economy*, London: Earthscan.

Pearson, K.R., Bäckman, M., Grenni, S., Morrigi, A., Pisters, S. and de Vrieze, A. (2018) *Arts-Based Methods for Transformative Engagement: A Toolkit*, Wageningen: SUSPLACE.

Pettit, P. (1997) *Republicanism: A Theory of Freedom and Government*, Oxford: Oxford University Press.

Pettit, P. (2014) *Just Freedom: A Moral Compass for a Complex World*, New York: W.W. Norton and Company.

Pierre, J. and Peters, B.G. (2000) *Governance, Politics and the State*, Basingstoke: Macmillan.

Pollitt, C. (2000) 'Is the emperor in his underwear? An analysis of the impacts of public management reform', *Public Management*, 2(2): 181–99.

Porter, M.E. (1998) *On Competition*, Boston: Harvard Business School Publishing.

Quinn, M. (1996) 'Central government planning policy', in Tewdwr-Jones, M. (ed) *British Planning Policy in Transition: Planning in the Major Years*, London: UCL Press, 17–30.

Quinn, M. (2000) 'Central government planning policy', in Prior, A., Raemaekers, J. and Allmendinger, P. (eds) *Introduction to Planning Practice*, Chichester: Wiley: 111–132.

Quinn, M. (2002) 'Evidence based or people based policy making? A view from Wales', *Public Policy and Administration*, 17(3): 29–42.

Quinn, M. (2018) *Building Successful Ecosystem Partnerships: A Report on Behalf of Welsh Government and Partners in the Brecon Beacons National Park*, Cardiff: Sustainable Places Research Institute, Cardiff University.

Quinn, M. and de Vrieze, A. (eds) (2019) *Creating Sustainable Places Together: A Quick Start Guide for Policy-makers and Practitioners to Place-based Working and Co-production*, Wageningen: Wageningen University and Research, SUSPLACE.

Resource Management Review Panel (2020) *New Directions for Resource Management in New Zealand*, Wellington: New Zealand Ministry of Environment.

Ringer, F.K. (2004) *Max Weber: An Intellectual Biography*, Chicago: University of Chicago Press.

RSPB (2013) *State of Nature*, Sandy: Royal Society for the Protection of Birds.

Savas, E.S. (1988) *Privatisation: The Key to Better Government*, Chatham: Chatham House Publishers.

Savoie, D.J. (1994) *Thatcher, Reagan & Mulroney: In Search of a New Bureaucracy*, Pittsburgh: University of Pittsburgh Press.

Seibel, W. (2010) 'Beyond bureaucracy: Public administration as political integrator and non-Weberian thought in Germany', *Public Administration Review*, 70(5): 719–30.

Sen, A. (1999) *Development as Freedom*, Oxford: Oxford University Press.

Simon, H.A. (1946) 'The proverbs of administration', *Public Administration Review*, 6(1): 53–67.

Simon, H.A. (1947) *Administrative Behavior: A Study of Decision-making Processes in Administrative Organisations*, New York: Macmillan.

Skyttner, L. (2005) *General Systems Theory: Problems, Perspectives, Practice*, 2nd edn, Singapore: World Scientific Publishing Co.

Smith, A. (2007) *An Inquiry into the Nature and Causes of the Wealth of Nations*, Wight, J.B. (ed), Petersfield: Harriman House Publishing.

Smith, G.H. (2012) *The System of Liberty: Themes in the History of Classical Liberalism*, New York: Cambridge University Press.

Steuart, J. (1767) *An Inquiry into the Principles of Political Oeconomy: Being an Essay on the Science of Domestic Policy in Free Nations. By Sir James Steuart, Bart*, London: printed for A. Millar, and T. Cadell, Eighteenth Century Collections Online.

Stoker, G. (1998) *Governance as Theory: Five Propositions, International Social Science Journal*, 50: 17–28.

Taylor, F.W. (1998) *The Principles of Scientific Management*, Mineola: Dover Publications.

Theriault, S.M. (2003) 'Patronage, the Pendleton Act, and the power of the people', *The Journal of Politics*, 65(1): 50–68.

Thompson, V.A. (1961) *Modern Organisation*, New York: Knopf.

Torfing, J. and Triantafillou, P. (2013) 'What's in a name? Grasping new public governance as a political-administrative system', *International Review of Public Administration*, 18(2): 9–25.

Torgerson, D. (2005) 'The ambivalence of discourse: Beyond the administrative mind?' in Paehlke, R. and Torgerson, D. (eds) *Managing Leviathan: Environmental Politics and the Administrative State*, 2nd edn, Toronto: University of Toronto Press, 97–124.

UK Government (1990) *This Common Inheritance: Britain's Environmental Strategy*, Cm 1200, London: HMSO.

United Nations (2015) *The Millennium Development Goals 2015*, New York: United Nations

United Nations Conference on Environment and Development (UNCED) (1992) *Agenda 21, Rio Declaration*, New York: United Nations.

United Nations Economic Commission for Europe (UNECE) (1998) *Aarhus Convention on Access to Information, Public Participation in Decision-making and Access to Justice in Environmental Matters*, Aarhus: UNECE.

Von Mises, L. (1944) *Bureaucracy*, New Haven: Yale University Press.

von Stein, L. (1958) *Verfaltungslehre und Verwaltungsrecht*, Frankfurt am Main: Vittorio Klostermann.

Voß, J.-P. and Bornemann, B. (2011) 'The politics of reflexive governance: Challenges for designing adaptive management and transition management', *Ecology and Society*, 16(2): 9.

Waldo, D. (1948) *The Administrative State: A Study of the Political Theory of American Public Administration*, New York: The Ronald Press Company.

Wallace, J. (2018) *Wellbeing and Devolution: Reframing the Role of Government in Scotland, Wales and Northern Ireland*, Cham: Palgrave Macmillan.

Waterman, R.W. and Meier, K.J. (1998) 'Principal-agent models: An expansion?', *Journal of Public Administration Research and Theory*, 8(2): 173–202.

Weber, M. (1922) *Wirtschaft und Gesellschaft*, Tübingen: Verlag von J C B Mohr (Paul Siebeck).

Weber, M. (1978) *Economy and Society: An Outline of Interpretive Sociology*, Roth, G. and Wittich, C. (eds), Berkeley and Los Angeles: University of California Press.

References

Weber, M. (2001) *The Protestant Ethic and the Spirit of Capitalism*, Parsons, T. (trans), London: Routledge.

Weil, S. (2002) *The Need for Roots: Prelude to a Declaration of Duties towards Mankind*, London and New York: Routledge.

Welsh Government (WG) (2004a) *Making the Connections: Delivering Better Services for Wales – The Welsh Assembly Government Vision for Public Services*, Cardiff: Welsh Assembly Government.

Welsh Government (WG) (2004b) *People Places Futures: The Wales Spatial Plan*, Cardiff: Welsh Assembly Government.

Welsh Government (WG) (2009) *One Wales: One Planet – The Sustainable Development Scheme of the Welsh Assembly Government*, Cardiff: Welsh Assembly Government.

Welsh Government (WG) (2012a) *Consultation Document: Proposals for a Sustainable Development Bill*, Cardiff: Welsh Government.

Welsh Government (WG) (2012b) *Practice Guidance – One Planet Development: Technical Advice Note 6 Planning for Sustainable Rural Communities*, Cardiff: Welsh Government.

Welsh Government (WG) (2014) *Commission on Public Service Governance and Delivery Summary Report*, Cardiff: Welsh Government.

Welsh Government (WG) (2016) *Taking Wales Forward: 2016–2021*, Cardiff: Welsh Government.

Welsh Government (WG) (2017a) *Prosperity for All: The National Strategy*, Cardiff: Welsh Government.

Welsh Government (WG) (2017b) *Prosperity for All: Economic Action Plan*, Cardiff: Welsh Government.

Welsh Government (WG) (2017c) *Natural Resources Policy*, Cardiff: Welsh Government.

Welsh Government (WG) (2018) *Planning Policy Wales, Edition 10*, Cardiff: Welsh Government.

Welsh Parliament (2021a) *Public Accounts Committee Inquiry: Barriers to the successful implementation of the Well-being of Future Generations (Wales) Act 2015 – Supporting Paper from Permanent Secretary (Welsh Government)*, 15 January. https://business.senedd.wales/documents/s112194/PAC5-04-21%20P2%20-%20Welsh%20Government.pdf

Welsh Parliament (2021b) *Delivering for Future Generations: The Story So Far*, Cardiff: Welsh Parliament Public Accounts Committee.

Wilson, W. (1887) 'The study of administration', *Political Science Quarterly*, 2(2): 197–222.

Wolfers, J. (2015) 'The dismal science: How economists came to dominate the conversation', *New York Times*, 23 January.

World Commission on Environment and Development (WCED) (1987) *Our Common Future*, Oxford: Oxford University Press.

Index

References to figures appear in *italic* type;
those in **bold** type refer to tables.

A

A Living Wales 69
Aarhus Convention 30
accountability and risk aversion 58
Anthropocene concept 8–9, 31
Arendt, Hannah 102
Armstrong, Robert 48
Audit Commission 57, 61
austerity 15, 51

B

'balancing' sustainability 30, 78
banking crisis 2008 26
Barry, John 9, 33
Berlin, Isaiah 66
biopower (*biopouvoir*) 6, 7, 22, 38, 97
Blühdorn, Ingolfur 37
Bolivia 70, 90, 117
Bornemann, Basil 100–1
bounded rationality 10, 16, 45, 55–7, 59,
    67, 78, 93, 111–12
Brandt Report 1980 28–9
Brundtland Report 1987
    civic republicanism echoes 9
    ethical mantra 29, 38, 101–2, 117
    governance, institutional change 31, 32, 33
    sustainable development agenda 29, 123
    Welsh Government's alignment 71, 73,
        75, 76, 77
bureaucratic experience,
        governmentality frame
    discipline 61–3
    institutional departmentalism 55–7, 62
    knowledge-power practices 52–3
    narratives, constraints 57–61
    territory, management of 53–5
bureaucratic practice
    Foucault's governmentality 40
    historic narratives, continuing
        influence 41–4
    Kammeralism 42–3
    managerialism 49–51, 57–8, 64, 95,
        115–16
    need for control 12–13, 64–5, 67, 93–5,
        111–12, 113
    public bureaucracy critiques 48–9, 123–4
    Waldo's critique 47–8
    Weber's characteristics and
        legitimacies 44–6, 48
    Wilson's public service goals 46–7

C

Canal & River Trust 83
capitalism 27, 37, 45, 67, 88, 123
Carson, Rachel 28
civic bureaucracy
    civic and ecological
        governmentality *96*, 96–7
    civic dialogue's importance 97, 102–3,
        105–7
    civic republicanism 99–100
    co-production/co-design 103–5, **105**,
        106, 107, 126–30
    constitutional approach 118–19
    funding/decision making
        processes 114–15
    key narratives and practices 97–9, **120**
    legal scope 105–7, 110–11, 112–13,
        114–15, 116, 118
    models and toolkits **120–2**
    non-domination ideal 99
    non-numerical data 112–13
    organization 115–16, **121**
    place, transformatory factors 107–10,
        109, 125–6
    public service concepts 113–15
    purpose and values 116–18, **122**
    system-wide, integrated changes 100–1
civic dialogue 33, 61, 65, 97, 102–7,
    106
civic republicanism
    civic dialogue 102, 103, 105
    criticisms 10
    enabling governance 66, 68, 95,
        107, 117
    green politics links 33
    guiding principles 9–10, 11, 123
    rule of law 10, 105, 119
civil service, UK 14–15, 17, 39–40, 43,
    48, 59–60, 140–2
Club of Rome 28
co-production/co-design 98, 103–5, **105**,
    106, 107, 126–30
Confederation of British Industry 87
competitive democracy 26, 37, 51, 58, 64,
    67, 80, 87, 99, 104, 107
complexity 32, 62, 64, 66 67, 98–99,
    112, **120**
constitutionalism and bureaucracy 10, 33,
    46, 47, 48, 70–71, 84, 89–90, 94, 110,
    116, 117, 118–19, *122*

Index

cost-benefit analysis 14, 52, 53, 94, 111, 112, 119, 120
Covid 19 pandemic 11, 26
creativity constraint 59
Cyfoeth Naturiol Cymru [Natural Resources Wales] 52–3, 69, 80
Cynnal Cymru- Sustain Wales 71

D

Davidson, Jane 69
Death, Carl 21
decentralization 19–20
Denhardt, Janet V. 51, 97
Denhardt, Robert B. 51, 97
Department of the Environment, UK 28, 29
departmentalism 55–7, 62, 115
discipline 7, 27, 40, 61–3, 64
Dobson, Andrew 8–9
domination and governance 7–8, 10–11, 19, 26–7, 37–8, 44 see also non-domination and governance
Drakeford, Mark 82
Dryzek, John 5, 102
Dylan, Bob 28

E

Earth Summit 2002 34–5
Earth System Governance Project 31–2
East India Company 43
Eckersley, Robyn 9, 33
ecological modernization 34, 35, 75, 95
ecologism 8–9
economics
  agglomeration model 54, 88, 91, **122**
  competition theory 8, 98, 117, **121**
  foundational economy 88–9, 98, 117
  growth 8–9, 25, 67, 75, 88, **122**
  heterodox economics 98, 117
  non-growth 37, 98, 117–118
  predominance 25, 111
  rational choice theory 98, 117
  time preference theory 52
efficiency and governance
  capitalist consumerism 27
  funding, proposal inflexibility 61–3
  historic narratives and values 42–3
  knowledge-power 11, 52–3
  land use planning, reform barriers 54–5, 109
  neoliberalism's impact 17, 26–7
  performance and decision metrics 61, 64–5, 95–6, 113
  prime narratives 9, 10, 25–7, 67, 93–5
Ecuador 90, 117
emancipatory promise 9, 12–13, 17, 19, 21, 23, 26, 33, 76, 93
Environment Agency 29

Environment (Wales) Act 2016 69, 72, 76–7, 80, 81, 89
Environment White Paper, UK 1990 29
Estonia 70
European Union (EU) 35, 70, 90

F

Forum for the Future 56
Foucault, Michel
  biopower (*biopouvoir*) 6, **7**, 22, 38, 97
  civic dialogue 103
  governance, purpose 5, 7–8, 18, 25
  governmentality 6–8, 7, 21, 27, 42, 51–52, 95, 109, 123
  knowledge-power 6, 11–12, 37–8, 40, 52–3, 98
  milieu 6, 15, 27, 33, 37, 40
  technologies of power 6–7, 37–8
foundational economy 88–9, 117
France 91
Franklin, Benjamin 10
freedom, concepts 9, 11
Future Generations Commissioners 71–72, 79–80, 85

G

Gauteng Declaration 35
Global South 17, 28
governance
  contextual meaning 18
  decentralization innovations 19–20
  delivery relationships 21–2
  institutional narratives 18–19
  participatory forms 20–1
governance, UK administration
  bureaucrats as agents 14–15, 48
  decentralization and devolution 19–20
  departmentalism barriers 55–7
  open network 15–16
  public service delivery, conceptual flaws 57–8
  socio-economic developments 16–17, 19
governance, US administration 10, 17, 46–7
governance, Welsh administration
  Audit Wales, role of 61–2, 81, 85
  economic strategy compromises 88–9
  funding, flexibility undermined 62–3, 85–6
  neutrality and creativity restrictions 59
  open network 16, 20
  participatory plans, implementation barriers 52–5, 57–8, 86
  partnership, practice failings 22–3
  social policies, reforms and constraints 23–5 see also see sustainable development – governance
  sustainable development schemes 35–7

government of the day 15, 46, 48, 60–1, 94
Government Office for the South-West 15, 20–1, 30
governmentality 6–8, 7, 18–19, 27, 34, 40, 42, 95, *96*, 123

H

Habermas, Jürgen 102, 103
Harrington, James 10
Heath, Joseph 97
hierarchies 22, 115
Hungary 70

I

Indigenous and local knowledge 32, 64, 99, 104, 111–112

J

Jennings, Bruce 33
jobs and growth narrative 26
Jones, Carwyn 26
Justi, Johann H.G. von 42–3

K

Kammeralism 42–3
Kelsall, Keith 40
knowledge-power 6, 11–12, 37–8, 40, 52–3, 98

L

Lafferty, William 37
land use planning, UK 53–5, 109, 110
Latin America 90–1
Leonard-Clarke, Willow 104–5
Local Agenda 21 30

M

Madison, James 10, 100
managerialism 23, 26, 49–50, 57–8, 64, 81–82, 86–87, 95
markets 22
Marx, Karl 39
Mayo, Elton 50
Meadowcroft, James 5, 67, 68
Meadows, Thomas Taylor 43
metagovernance 113, 116
metric power 52, 53, 65
milieu
  bureaucratic practices 37, 40, 53, 61
  contextual meaning 6, 15, 27
  governance role 33, 37, 67, 95–6
Mill, John Stuart 26–7, 118
Mills, C. Wright 112
mimetics 41, 95
Montesquieu 10, 48, 96, 118
Morgan, Rhodri 19, 23, 24, 35, 58

N

National Assembly for Wales, formation 16, 68
National Economic Development Council 19
nationalism, growth of 11–12
Natural Resources Wales [Cyfoeth Naturiol Cymru] 52–3, 69, 80, 82, 89
neoliberalism 4, 12, 17, 19–20, 23, 24, 26–7, 41, 48, 50, 64
networks 14–15, 20–1, 22
neutrality 10, 48, 59, 74, 94, 97, 117
New Labour 56
New Public Administration 48
New Public Governance 50, 98, 113–14, 116
New Public Management
  controlling mantra 22, 24, 41, 95, 113
  key focus and arguments 50–1
  public service delivery impact 57–8
  Welsh Government push back 23–5
New Public Service 33, 98, 114
New Zealand 90, 91
Niskanen, William A. 49
non-domination and governance
  civic bureaucracy 99–101
  civic republicanism 9–10, 99–100, 123
  ecological argument 8–9
  Sen's approach 30
  Well-being Act (Wales) 72–3, 76, 77–8, 80–2
non-governmental organizations (NGOs) 21, 30, 58, 63, 71, 86–87
non-numerical data 53, 111–13
Northcote, Stafford 43

O

One Planet Living 55
One Wales: One Planet 36, 69
organization theory 49–50, 98
Ostrom, Elinor 102, 109

P

participatory governance 14–15, 20–1, 65–6
Pearce, David 30
Pettit, Phillip 5, 9, 76, 80, 99–100, 102, 119
place-based governance
  landscape-scale partnership 82, 104–5, **106**, 109–10, *109*
  localized processes 110–11
  systematic barriers 54–5, 109, 110
  transformatory factors 32–3, 107–8
Plaid Cymru 86–7
Planning (Wales) Act 2015 72, 81, 89

Index

Pluralism 10, 11, 45, 47, 58, 66, 67, 78, 97, 101, 102
political economy 6, 13, 25, 37, 42, 43, 52, 59, 88–89, 118
Porter, Michael 26
Project Skyline 62, 82
public bureaucracy 46–7, 48–9, 60
public service delivery, flaws 57–8
public value theory 107, 113–14, 116

Q

Quebec 70
Quinn, Matthew 13–16, 30, 39–40, 56, 118

R

rational choice theory 23, 113
Reaganomics 17
reflexivity 13, 32, 51, 53, 61, 63, 65, 66, 67, 81, 92, 93, 96–97, 108, 112, 114–116, **120, 122**
regimes of truth 6, 12, 38, 95
right populism 11–12, 96
Ringer, Fritz K. 45
Rio Earth Summit 1992 29, 30
Royal Commission on Environmental Pollution (RCEP) 57
rule of law 9, 10, 46, 105, 119

S

Sargeant, Carl 81
Savas, E.S. 21–2
scientific management 49–50
Sen, Amartya 30
Simon, Herbert, A. 49, 115
Smith, Adam 42
social contract theory 33
societal self-steering 32, 33, 38
stakeholder/s 14–15, 21
Steuart, James 42
Stockholm Declaration 1972 28
strong sustainability 30
supply-side economics 17
sustainable development
  civic republicanism links 9–10
  concept origins 27–8
  contested adoption 17, 31, 37–8, 92
  deliberative/discursive governance 32–33, 61, 65, 90, 102, 107, 125
  enabling governance 97–98, 113–114, 116, 123
  governance, forms of change 31–2
  governance *of* 34–5, 37–8
  governing *for* 32–4, 38
  international mechanisms 28–30
  key relevance 31
  legal rights innovations, national 70, 90
Sustainable Development Commission, UK 57
Sustainable Development Goals 35, 44, 70

sustainable development, UK policy 30, 35–7, 54–5, 55–7
sustainable development, Welsh governance
  auditing powers 81, 85
  bureaucratic practice changes 83
  Commissioner, appointment and role 69–70, 71, 72, 79–80, 85, 87
  flexible bureaucracy 81–2
  historical context 68
  landscape-scale initiatives 82
  place-based representation 72, 78–9, 80, 81, 82
  strategy challenges 8–9, 87–9
  Well-being Act, framework values and purpose 73–6, 73–4, 81–2
  Well-being Act, legislative weaknesses 84–6
  Well-being Act, lobbied criticisms 86–7
  Well-being Act, principle and behaviours **77–8**, 77–8, 80
  Well-being of Future Generations (Wales) Act 2015 69–72
systems thinking 8, 11, 32, 67, 76, 98, 108, 112, 121, **122**

T

Taylor, F.W. 49
technocracy 27, 35, 37, 42, 59, 67, 78, 97, 103, **120**
technologies of power 5, 6, 8, 9, 13, 34, 37–8, 97, 108–109
territory 7, 38, 42, 53–5, 91–2
Thatcherism 17
Thompson, Victor A. 49
time preference theory 52
Torgerson, Douglas 42
transition/transformation 33
Transport for Wales 82
Trevelyan, George Otto 43
'Type II partnerships' 34–5

U

uncertainty 32, 38, 61, 67, 81, 99, 112, 115
uniformity 8, 11, 13, 45, 47, 54–55, 57, 63, 64, 67, 96–97, 100–101, 107–111
unlearning 53, 112
United Nations (UN) 21, 28, 30, 35, 44, 70
United States (US) 10, 90, 118–19
unsustainability, politics of 37

V

Valleys Task Force 82
Von Mises, Ludwig 48–9
Von Stein, Lorenz 46
Voß, Jan-Peter 100–1

W

Waldo, Dwight 47–8, 49, 50
Wales Spatial Plan 23, 36, 54–5
Wales We Want, The 71, 87
WCED *see* Brundtland Report
weak sustainability 30
Weber, Max 5, 7, 43, 44–6, 52, 96, 97
Weil, Simone 108
welfare state 17, 19, 50
Well-being of Future Generations (Wales)
    Act 2015
  bureaucratic practice changes 83
  consultation process 70–1, 87
  criticisms and challenges 86–7
  departmental response, example 131
  guiding focus 69–70, 117
  economic strategy compromises 88–9
  Future Generations Commissioner
    79–80, 82
  legally binding goals 71
  legislative weaknesses 84–5, 89–90

narrative goals, emancipatory and
    egalitarian 73–6, 81–2, 84
new initiatives generated 82–3
non-domination principles 72–3
planning tensions 89
Public Accounts Committee Inquiry,
    written evidence 132–9
Public Service Boards 72, 78–9, 80, 81,
    82, 87
scope and responsibilities 72, 81, 83–4
strategy precursors 69
sustainable development principle 77–8
sustainable development schemes 36–7
title change decisions 71–2
Welsh Government *see* governance,
    Welsh administration
Welsh Senate Public Accounts Committee
    report 83, 85
Welsh Water- Dwr Cymru 82
Williams Commission 2014 25
Wilson, Woodrow 5, 14, 46–7, 51, 65, 93